CONSTRUCTION MANAGEMENT MADE EASY

A PRACTICAL GUIDE FOR OWNERS MANAGERS AND STUDENTS

SECOND EDITION

The ultimate self-help guide and handbook for understanding the essentials of do-it-yourself construction management clear, practical, and adaptable for projects of any size.

By

W. GARY WESTERNOFF

CONSTRUCTION MANAGEMENT MADE EASY

A Practical Guide for Owners, Managers, and Students

Second Edition

ISBN (Paper Back): 978-0-9668245-2-0

ISBN (eBook): 978-0-9668245-3-7

Library of Congress Control Number: 2026907828

Published by Ponta Inc. (DBA Constructionplace.com)

P.O. Box 153
Moraga, CA 94556

Printed in the United States of America

Editor: W. Gary Westernoff
Worksheets and Templates: W. Gary Westernoff

About the Author

W. Gary Westernoff is the Founder and President of Ponta Inc. and Constructionplace.com, a pioneering platform dedicated to empowering owners, improving project outcomes, and bringing clarity to the construction process. With college degrees in Architecture and Construction Management (DAI), Gary combines technical training with decades of hands-on experience in general contracting, project management, and owner representation.

A U.S. Army veteran, Past Commander of VFW Post 1540 in Honolulu, Shriner, and Past President of the Lamorinda, California Rotary Club, Gary brings a disciplined, service-driven approach to leadership, communication, and community engagement. His work blends practical field experience with strategic insight, resulting in tools, frameworks, and educational resources that are accessible, actionable, and grounded in real-world practice.

Gary is the creator of the Magic Budget Calculator, an AI-powered planning tool that helps owners understand costs, forecast budgets, and make informed decisions before engaging contractors. He is also the author of Construction Management Made Easy and co-author of Construction Like Sushi, both of which reflect his commitment to clear communication, owner education, and innovative teaching methods.

Through Constructionplace.com, Gary continues to develop tools, templates, and guidance that support owners, builders, educators, and professionals around the world. Driven by a belief that construction should be transparent, predictable, and collaborative, his work focuses on empowering owners with the knowledge and structure they need to lead successful projects from start to finish.

DISCLOSURE AND BOOK LIMITATIONS

The information in this book is based on the author's training, professional experience, and decades of practical involvement in construction and construction management. Neither the author nor the publisher offers legal advice or guidance in other licensed professional disciplines. Readers should consult properly qualified professionals—such as attorneys, architects, engineers, or accountants whenever specialized advice is required.

Some examples in this book reference the California Contractors' License Law. These examples may not apply in other states or jurisdictions, as construction statutes and requirements vary widely. Readers should verify all legal forms including Waiver and Release forms, lien documents, and contract templates with qualified legal professionals in the geographical area where their project is located.

This book is intended as a practical guide to help owners, managers, and students better understand construction processes and terminology. It is not a substitute for professional services, nor does it replace the need for competent legal, technical, or financial advice when undertaking a construction project. Constructionplace.com is referenced throughout this book as a supporting resource, though the author cannot guarantee its ongoing availability or operation.

Table of Contents

Foreword

This book was written for every owner, builder, and decision-maker who has ever felt overwhelmed by the construction process. After decades in the field, I've seen the same pattern repeat itself: good people making costly mistakes simply because the information they needed wasn't clear, accessible, or organized in a way they could actually use.

Construction doesn't have to be confusing. It doesn't have to be adversarial. And it certainly doesn't have to drain time, money, or trust. When owners understand the process, they gain control. When expectations are clear, projects stay on track. When everyone knows their role, the work becomes predictable even enjoyable.

This book is my contribution to that clarity. It distills a lifetime of lessons into practical guidance owners can rely on. My hope is that it helps you approach your next project with confidence, insight, and the tools to make smart decisions from day one.

Preface to the Second Edition

Construction has changed dramatically since this book first appeared in 1998 — but the core challenge facing owners has not. Whether the project is a simple remodel, a major renovation, or a complex building upgrade, owners still struggle with the same questions: Where do I start? Who can I trust? How do I control costs? How do I avoid mistakes that others have already made?

When I wrote the first edition, my goal was simple: give everyday people the tools, confidence, and practical knowledge to manage their own projects successfully. I wanted to demystify the process, expose the pitfalls, and show that construction management is not an exclusive club reserved for professionals. With the right guidance, anyone can lead a project with clarity and control.

That mission has only grown more important. Today, owners face rising construction costs, complex building systems, new sustainability requirements, and an industry that often benefits when owners remain uninformed. At the same time, technology has opened the door to smarter planning, better communication, and more transparent decision-making. Owners now have access to tools and resources that simply didn't exist when the first edition was published.

This Second Edition reflects all of that progress. It expands the original content with modern best practices, updated standards, and new chapters on sustainability, affordable housing, plumbing and building systems, condo governance, and owner-led project oversight. It integrates digital tools, checklists, and templates from Constructionplace.com — a platform I created to give owners, managers, and professionals a practical, affordable way to plan, budget, and manage projects from start to finish.

But the heart of this book remains the same: empower the owner. You will not find academic theory here. You will find real-world guidance, step-by-step processes, and proven methods developed over decades of hands-on experience as a builder, design-builder, instructor, consultant, and advocate for owner rights and transparent governance. My goal is to help you avoid unnecessary costs, prevent experience level.

If you are an amateur, this book will give you clarity.

If you are a professional, it will sharpen your process. avoidable mistakes, and manage your project with confidence no matter your background or

If you are a board member or property manager, it will raise your standards.

If you are a student, it will give you a foundation that will serve you throughout your career.

Most importantly, if you are an owner, this book will give you control.

Thank you for joining me in this Second Edition. I hope it serves you well, saves you time and money, and helps you deliver a successful project the easy way.

W Gary Westernoff, Author

For Instructors and Educators

This book was written for owners, board members, managers, and anyone who wants to take control of their construction projects. But it is also designed to support instructors who teach construction management, project planning, and building stewardship in classrooms, workshops, and professional training programs over the structured learning environment. Students gain confidence. Instructors gain clarity. And future owners, managers, and community leaders gain a practical foundation they can use throughout their careers.

To make this book easy to teach, a stand-alone Instructor's Guide is available in Appendix C. It includes sample syllabi, weekly learning objectives, assignments, case studies, quizzes, and teaching tools that align directly with the chapters in this book. Whether you are teaching a 4-week workshop, an 8 or 12-week professional course, or a full 16-week semester, the guide provides a flexible framework you ca n adopt or adapt to your program.

My hope is that this material helps instructors bring real-world construction management into the classroom in a way that is simple, practical, and empowering.

Thank you for choosing to teach with this book and for helping prepare the next generation of owners, managers, and stewards of our built environment.

Getting Started

"Construction Management" is a broad term often used to describe the process of organizing and directing labor, materials, and equipment to achieve the designer's intent. "Project Management," on the other hand, focuses on coordinating time, money, tasks, equipment, and people. In practice, these two terms are frequently used interchangeably.

This book focuses on Construction Management the practical, day-to-day leadership required to plan, organize, and successfully complete a construction project.

A natural question arises:

Where do you fit into the Construction Management process?

To help readers understand their starting point, the author has identified several classifications. Many individuals fall into more than one.

Where do you fit into the total scheme of the Construction Management Process?

Amateur

Someone who attempts construction-related tasks without formal training—often motivated by interest, curiosity, or necessity.

Desperate

A person forced into a construction project under urgent conditions. Examples include a leaking roof, plumbing failure, a broken water heater, a collapsing retaining wall, or any situation where immediate action is required. Desperation often leads to rushed decisions and costly mistakes.

Novice

A beginner with little or no experience in construction or project management.

Owner's Representative

A person hired by the owner to manage day-to-day construction activities on their behalf. Titles may include project manager, construction manager, project engineer, or facilities manager. Responsibilities often include budgeting, estimating, planning, quality control, specification compliance, and approving contractor payments.

Professional

A person or company formally trained, licensed, or experienced in a construction-related profession.

Student

An individual studying construction management or a related field in a school, college, or university.

Determining Your Classification

Using the definitions above, check the classification(s) that best describe your background or experience in Construction Management:

_______ Amateur

_______ Desperate

_______ Novice

_______ Owner's Representative

_______ Professional

_______ Student

Recommended Reading Path

If you checked Amateur, Novice, or Student:

The author recommends the following study sequence:

1. Chapter 1 - Owner as Project Leader
2. Chapter 2 - Understanding the Construction Project
3. Chapter 9 - Hiring Designers, Contractors & Consultants
4. Chapter 11 - Communication & Documentation
5. Chapter 10 - Contracts that protect you
6. Chapter 18 - Project Management Tools & Templates

If you checked Desperate:

Start with the sections most likely to help you make immediate, informed decisions:

1. Chapter 15 – Remodeling, Repairs & Emergency Projects
2. Chapter 3 - Essential Tools for Every Project
3. Chapter 9 - Hiring Designers, Contractors & Consultants
4. Chapter 10 - Contracts that protect you
5. Chapter 18 - Project Management Tools & Templates

If you checked Owner's Representative or Professional:

This book serves as a practical reference guide and handbook. The forms, checklists, and glossary are designed to help you organize, standardize, and strengthen your existing policies, procedures, and terminology.

Chapter 1 — The Owner as Project Leader

Construction projects succeed or fail long before the first hammer swings. They succeed when the owner understands their role, sets the direction, and leads with clarity. They fail when the owner steps back, assumes others will "handle it," or allows the process to drift without structure or accountability.

This chapter establishes the foundation for everything that follows. Whether you are an amateur, a seasoned professional, a condo board member, or a property manager, your leadership determines the outcome. You don't need to be a contractor or an engineer. You simply need to understand the process, make informed decisions, and guide the team with purpose.

1.1 Why the Owner Matters More Than Anyone Else

Every construction project has many players — architects, engineers, contractors, inspectors, suppliers, and consultants. Each has a role, but none has the full picture. Only the owner sees the entire project from concept to completion. Only the owner defines success.

When owners lead effectively:

- Costs stay under control
- Schedules remain realistic
- Quality improves
- Communication stays clear
- Problems are resolved early
- The team works together instead of against each other

When owners do not lead:

- Scope drifts
- Budgets explode
- Contractors make assumptions
- Designers over-specify
- Delays multiply
- Mistakes go unnoticed until they are expensive to fix

Leadership is not about doing the work — it's about directing it.

1.2 What It Means to Be a Project Leader

Being a project leader does not mean:

- Becoming a construction expert
- Micromanaging the contractor
- Doing the work yourself
- Being on site every day

It does mean:

- Setting clear goals
- Making timely decisions
- Establishing accountability

- Keeping communication structured
- Using checklists, logs, and tools
- Asking the right questions at the right time

A project leader is a coordinator, not a technician. You guide the process, not the hammer.

1.3 The Phased Approach: Your Most Powerful Tool

Most owners get overwhelmed because they try to think about everything at once. The solution is simple: break the project into phases and focus on one phase at a time.

The phases are:

1. Concept & Feasibility
2. Planning & Pre-Construction
3. Design & Documentation
4. Bidding & Procurement
5. Construction
6. Closeout & Post-Construction

Each phase has its own decisions, checklists, and deliverables. You never move to the next phase until the current one is complete. This prevents rework, surprises, and unnecessary costs.

This book — and Constructionplace.com — are built around this phased method because it works for every project, every budget, and every experience level.

1.4 The Three Core Responsibilities of Every Owner

1. Define the Project

You decide what you want, why you want it, and what success looks like. No one else can do this for you.

2. Build the Right Team

You select the designer, contractor, and consultants. You set expectations. You require transparency and competitive pricing.

3. Manage the Process

You keep the project aligned with your goals. You approve changes. You track progress. You ensure accountability.

If you do these three things well, the rest of the project becomes dramatically easier.

1.5 Common Mistakes Owners Make — and How to Avoid Them

Mistake 1: Starting construction before planning is complete

This leads to change orders, delays, and cost overruns.

Solution: Complete each phase before moving on.

Mistake 2: Relying too heavily on one person
No single contractor or designer should control the entire project.

Solution: Maintain balanced oversight and clear documentation.

Mistake 3: Not documenting decisions
Verbal agreements disappear when problems arise.

Solution: Use logs, checklists, and written approvals.

Mistake 4: Avoiding tough questions
Owners sometimes hesitate to ask for clarification.

Solution: Ask early, ask often, and never assume.

Mistake 5: Not understanding the contract
Contracts protect the contractor unless the owner understands them.

Solution: Learn the key clauses — this book will show you how.

1.6 Tools That Make You a Stronger Leader

You don't need to invent your own systems. Use:

- Checklists
- Budget worksheets
- Schedules
- Meeting logs
- Communication templates
- Change order forms
- Inspection checklists

These tools keep you organized and keep the team accountable. They also reduce stress, confusion, and costly misunderstandings.

Constructionplace.com provides digital versions of these tools so you can manage your project from anywhere.

1.7 Leadership Without Stress

Many owners' fear construction because they've heard horror stories. But most problems come from:

- Poor planning
- Weak communication
- Lack of documentation

- Unclear expectations

When you lead with structure, the stress disappears. You don't need to know everything — you just need a system. This book gives you that system.

1.8 Your Role Throughout the Book

As you move through the chapters, you will learn:

- What decisions you must make
- What questions to ask
- What documents to require
- What pitfalls to avoid
- What tools to use
- How to stay in control

By the end, you will be able to manage any project — confidently, efficiently, and without unnecessary cost.

Chapter 2 — Understanding the Construction Process

Most construction problems begin with misunderstanding. Owners often assume the process is linear, predictable, and controlled by the contractor. In reality, construction is a coordinated sequence of decisions, documents, approvals, and responsibilities — and the owner sits at the center of it all.

This chapter gives you a clear, simplified roadmap of the entire process. Once you understand how the pieces fit together, you'll be able to lead your project with confidence, anticipate issues before they arise, and communicate effectively with every member of your team.

2.1 The Construction Process at a Glance

Every project — from a small remodel to a major building upgrade — follows the same general flow:

1. Concept & Feasibility
2. Planning & Pre-Construction
3. Design & Documentation
4. Bidding & Procurement
5. Construction
6. Closeout & Post-Construction

These phases overlap slightly, but each has its own purpose, deliverables, and decisions. Skipping or rushing any phase increases cost, risk, and stress.

2.2 Phase 1 — Concept & Feasibility

This is where your project begins — not with drawings, not with contractors, but with clarity.

You define:

- What you want
- Why you want it
- What constraints you face
- What success looks like

Feasibility includes:

- Rough budget expectations
- Basic schedule considerations
- Site or building limitations
- Regulatory or HOA constraints
- Early risk identification

This phase prevents unrealistic expectations and costly surprises later.

2.3 Phase 2 — Planning & Pre-Construction

This is the most important phase of the entire project. The more you plan, the less you pay.

Key tasks include:

- Establishing your budget
- Creating a preliminary schedule
- Identifying required consultants
- Gathering existing drawings and records
- Conducting site inspections
- Defining scope in detail
- Setting communication and documentation systems

This is also where you begin using tools such as:

- Checklists
- Logs
- Budget worksheets
- Meeting templates
- Constructionplace.com planning tools

A well-planned project is a predictable project.

2.4 Phase 3 — Design & Documentation

Design is not just about aesthetics — it's about clarity, coordination, and cost control.

This phase includes:

- Conceptual design
- Schematic design
- Design development
- Construction documents
- Engineering coordination
- Specifications

Good design reduces change orders, delays, and disputes. Poor design guarantees them.

Your role:

- Approve each design stage
- Ensure the design matches your goals and budget
- Ask questions early
- Require clarity before moving forward

Design is where most owners lose control — but with structure, you stay in charge.

2.5 Phase 4 — Bidding & Procurement

This is where you select the contractor or team that will build your project.

The process includes:

- Preparing bid packages
- Soliciting competitive bids
- Reviewing proposals
- Checking references
- Evaluating qualifications
- Negotiating terms
- Awarding the contract

Competitive bidding protects you from inflated pricing and hidden assumptions. Even in design-build or negotiated contracts, transparency is essential.

Your role:

- Require apples-to-apples bids
- Ask for clarifications in writing

- Compare scope, exclusions, and assumptions
- Select based on value, not just price

A well-run bidding process sets the tone for the entire project

2.6 Phase 5 — Construction

This is the visible phase — but it's not where leadership begins. By the time construction starts, your planning and documentation should be complete.

Construction includes:

- Mobilization
- Site preparation
- Structural work
- Mechanical, electrical, and plumbing systems
- Finishes
- Inspections
- Progress payments
- Change orders
- Quality control

Your role:

- Attend scheduled meetings
- Review progress reports
- Approve changes only when justified
- Track schedule and budget
- Maintain documentation
- Hold the team accountable

Construction is where strong owners shine — not by micromanaging, but by staying informed and structured.

2.7 Phase 6 — Closeout & Post-Construction

Many owners underestimate this phase, but it's critical to long-term success.

Closeout includes:

- Punch lists
- Final inspections
- As-built drawings
- Warranties

- O&M manuals
- Final payments
- Retainage release

Post-construction includes:

- Warranty tracking
- Maintenance planning
- Long-term asset management

A project is not complete until you have everything you need to operate, maintain, and protect your investment.

2.8 How the Phases Work Together

Each phase builds on the previous one. When you complete each phase fully before moving on:

- Costs stay predictable
- Schedules stay realistic
- Quality improves
- Stress decreases
- Disputes are minimized

When phases overlap too much or are rushed:

- Change orders multiply
- Delays increase
- Budgets explode
- Mistakes become expensive

Your discipline is the key to project success.

2.9 The Owner's Role Throughout the Process

Across all phases, your responsibilities remain consistent:

- Define the project
- Build the right team
- Manage the process
- Document decisions
- Ask questions early
- Stay organized

You don't need to be a construction expert — you just need a system. This book gives you that system.

2.10 Why Understanding the Process Protects You

When you understand the process:

- You make better decisions
- You avoid unnecessary costs
- You prevent scope creep
- You maintain control
- You communicate with confidence
- You hold the team accountable

Knowledge is your greatest protection — and your greatest advantage.

Chapter 3 — Essential Tools for Every Project

Construction is not complicated because the work is difficult — it's complicated because the information is scattered. Projects fall apart when decisions aren't documented, communication isn't structured, and no one knows who said what, when, or why. The right tools solve that problem.

This chapter introduces the essential tools every owner needs to manage a project with confidence. These tools don't require special training, expensive software, or industry experience. They simply provide structure — and structure is what keeps your project on track.

3.1 Why Tools Matter More Than Experience

You don't need to be a contractor to manage a project well. You just need:

- A clear process
- A way to track decisions
- A way to communicate consistently
- A way to document progress
- A way to hold people accountable

Tools give you all of that.

Professionals use tools because they work. Owners should too.

3.2 The Core Tool Categories

Every project, regardless of size, needs tools in these categories:

1. Planning Tools
2. Budgeting Tools
3. Scheduling Tools
4. Communication Tools

5. Documentation Tools
6. Quality Control Tools
7. Change Management Tools
8. Closeout Tools

You don't need dozens of forms — just the right ones, used consistently.

3.3 Planning Tools

Planning tools help you define your project clearly before spending money.

Essential planning tools include:

- Project Definition Worksheet
- Scope Checklist
- Feasibility Checklist
- Risk Identification Worksheet
- Existing Conditions Checklist

These tools prevent unrealistic expectations and help you avoid surprises later.

3.4 Budgeting Tools

Budgeting is where most owners lose control. A good budgeting system keeps you grounded and prevents overspending.

Essential budgeting tools include:

- Master Budget Worksheet
- Cost Breakdown Structure (CBS)
- Allowance and Contingency Tracker
- Payment Log
- Magic Budget Calculator (online tool)

A budget is not a guess — it's a living document that evolves as the project becomes clearer.

3.5 Scheduling Tools

A schedule is more than dates — it's a roadmap for decision-making.

Essential scheduling tools include:

- Milestone Schedule
- Critical Path Checklist
- Decision Deadline Tracker
- Inspection and Permit Timeline

A good schedule prevents delays, reduces stress, and keeps the team aligned.

3.6 Communication Tools

Construction communication must be structured. Verbal agreements lead to disputes. Written communication protects you.

Essential communication tools include:

- Meeting Agenda Template
- Meeting Minutes Log
- Weekly Progress Report Template
- RFI (Request for Information) Log
- Decision Log

These tools ensure that everyone knows what was discussed, what was decided, and what comes next.

3.7 Documentation Tools

Documentation is your insurance policy. If it's not documented, it didn't happen.

Essential documentation tools include:

- Document Control Log
- Drawing and Revision Log
- Submittal Log
- Permit and Inspection Log
- Daily Site Report Template

These tools keep your project organized and protect you in case of disputes.

3.8 Quality Control Tools

Quality is not something you "hope for." It's something you verify.

Essential quality control tools include:

- Inspection Checklists (by trade)
- Punch List Template
- Material Verification Log
- Workmanship Standards Checklist

These tools help you confirm that the work meets your expectations and the contract requirements.

3.9 Change Management Tools

Changes are inevitable — but chaos is not.

Essential change management tools include:

- Change Order Request Form
- Change Order Log
- Cost Impact Worksheet
- Schedule Impact Worksheet

These tools prevent surprises and help you make informed decisions.

3.10 Closeout Tools

Closeout is where many projects fall apart. Without structure, you end up with missing documents, unresolved issues, and no protection.

Essential closeout tools include:

- Final Punch List
- Warranty Log
- As-Built Documentation Checklist
- O&M (Operating and Maintenance) Manual Checklist
- Final Payment Checklist

A project is not complete until closeout is complete.

3.11 Digital Tools and Online Platforms

Today's owners have access to tools that didn't exist when the first edition was written. Digital tools make it easier to:

- Track budgets
- Manage documents
- Communicate with the team
- Store photos and reports
- Access checklists and templates
- Collaborate remotely

Constructionplace.com integrates many of these tools into a single, easy-to-use platform designed specifically for owners, managers, and professionals.

3.12 How to Use These Tools Effectively

Tools only work when used consistently. Here's how to get the most out of them:

- Use the same forms throughout the project
- Keep everything in one place
- Update logs immediately after decisions
- Share documents with the team

- Review tools at each phase transition
- Use checklists before approving anything

Consistency is more important than complexity.

3.13 The Tools You'll Use Throughout This Book

As you move through the chapters, you'll see references to:

- Checklists
- Worksheets
- Logs
- Templates
- Online tools
- Standards and guidelines

These tools are included in the appendices and available online so you can use them immediately.

3.14 Tools Turn Chaos into Clarity

Construction becomes overwhelming when information is scattered. Tools bring order to the process. They help you:

- Stay organized
- Communicate clearly
- Track progress
- Control costs
- Prevent disputes
- Make informed decisions

Tools are the backbone of successful construction management — and they are the reason this book is called Construction Management Made Easy.

Chapter 4 — Defining Your Project

Every successful construction project begins long before drawings, bids, or contracts. It begins with clarity. Owners often rush into design or hire contractors before they fully understand what they want, why they want it, and what constraints they face. This leads to scope creep, budget overruns, delays, and frustration.

Defining your project is the single most important step in the entire process. It sets the direction, establishes expectations, and becomes the foundation for planning, design, budgeting, and construction. Without a clear definition, the project will drift. With one, everything becomes easier.

This chapter gives you the tools and structure to define your project with confidence.

4.1 Why Project Definition Matters

A well-defined project:

- Reduces uncertainty
- Prevents misunderstandings
- Controls costs
- Speeds up decision-making
- Improves design quality
- Strengthens bidding accuracy
- Minimizes change orders

A poorly defined project does the opposite. It creates confusion, invites assumptions, and forces the team to guess — and guessing is expensive.

Project definition is not optional. It is the foundation of everything that follows

4.2 The Four Pillars of Project Definition

Every project, regardless of size or complexity, must be defined in four key areas:

1. Purpose — Why are you doing this project?
2. Scope — What exactly are you building or improving?
3. Constraints — What limits or conditions must be respected?
4. Success Criteria — How will you know the project is successful?

These pillars guide every decision you make.

4.3 Defining the Purpose

Purpose is the "why" behind your project. It influences design, budget, schedule, and priorities.

Common project purposes include:

- Improving functionality
- Increasing property value
- Reducing maintenance costs
- Enhancing safety
- Meeting regulatory requirements
- Upgrading outdated systems
- Creating new space
- Improving energy efficiency
- Preparing for future needs

When the purpose is clear, decisions become easier. When it's vague, the project becomes vulnerable to unnecessary complexity and cost.

4.4 Defining the Scope

Scope is the "what" of your project — the specific work to be performed.

Scope includes:

- Spaces to be remodeled or built
- Systems to be upgraded (plumbing, electrical, HVAC)
- Materials and finishes
- Structural changes
- Code or safety improvements
- Accessibility upgrades
- Sustainability features
- Optional enhancements

Scope must be detailed, not general. "Remodel the kitchen" is not a scope. "Replace cabinets, countertops, appliances, flooring, lighting, and plumbing fixtures" is.

The more specific your scope, the more accurate your budget and bids will be.

4.5 Defining Constraints

Every project has constraints. Ignoring them leads to delays, redesigns, and cost overruns.

Common constraints include:

- Budget — Your financial limit
- Schedule — Deadlines, occupancy needs, seasonal factors
- Site or building conditions — Existing structure, utilities, access
- Regulatory requirements — Permits, codes, HOA (Home Owners Association) rules
- Operational needs — Working in occupied spaces
- Logistics — Staging areas, noise limits, delivery restrictions
- Design limitations — Structural or mechanical realities

Constraints are not obstacles — they are parameters that guide smart decision-making.

4.6 Defining Success Criteria

Success criteria answer the question: How will I know this project was successful?

Success criteria may include:

- Staying within budget
- Meeting the schedule
- Achieving a specific quality level
- Reducing long-term maintenance
- Improving energy efficiency
- Enhancing safety or accessibility
- Minimizing disruption
- Achieving a specific aesthetic

Success criteria keep the team aligned and prevent scope creep.

4.7 Tools for Defining Your Project

Use structured tools to capture your project definition clearly and consistently.

Essential tools include:

- Project Definition Worksheet
- Scope Checklist
- Purpose Statement Template
- Constraint Identification Worksheet
- Success Criteria Checklist
- Existing Conditions Checklist

These tools ensure nothing is overlooked and help you communicate clearly with designers and contractors.

4.8 The Importance of Existing Conditions

Before defining scope, you must understand what already exists. Existing conditions influence cost, design, and feasibility.

Key existing conditions to document:

- Structural elements
- Plumbing systems
- Electrical systems
- Mechanical systems
- Building envelope
- Accessibility
- Code compliance
- Previous modifications
- Hidden conditions (as much as possible)

Ignoring existing conditions is one of the most common — and costly — mistakes owners make.

4.9 Aligning Your Project with Your Budget

Your project definition must align with your financial reality. This doesn't mean compromising quality — it means making informed decisions.

To align scope and budget:

- Prioritize must-haves vs. nice-to-haves
- Identify cost drivers early
- Use allowances wisely
- Build in contingencies
- Use the Magic Budget Calculator for early estimates

A realistic budget is a powerful decision-making tool.

4.10 Aligning Your Project with Your Schedule

Your schedule effects:

- Costs
- Contractor availability
- Material lead times
- Occupancy needs
- Seasonal conditions
- Permit timelines

Define your schedule early to avoid surprises later.

4.11 Communicating Your Project Definition

Once your project is defined, communicate it clearly to:

- Designers
- Engineers
- Contractors
- Consultants
- Stakeholders
- Board members (for condo/HOA projects)

Clear communication prevents misunderstandings and ensures everyone is working toward the same goal.

4.12 Updating Your Project Definition as Needed

Project definition is not static. It evolves as you learn more. Update it when:

- New information emerges
- Constraints change
- Budget or schedule shifts
- Scope becomes clearer

But update it before design or construction begins — not during.

4.13 A Well-Defined Project Saves Time, Money, and Stress

When your project is clearly defined:

- Designers produce better drawings
- Contractors submit more accurate bids
- Change orders decrease
- Delays are minimized
- Communication improves
- Decisions become easier
- The project stays aligned with your goals

Project definition is the foundation of construction management made easy.

Chapter 5 — Budgeting Made Easy

Budgeting is where most construction projects succeed or fail. Owners often underestimate costs, overlook hidden expenses, or rely on rough guesses instead of structured planning. The result is predictable: cost overruns, stress, delays, and difficult decisions made under pressure.

A good budget is not a spreadsheet — it is a management tool. It guides decisions, sets expectations, and keeps the project aligned with your goals. When your budget is clear, realistic, and updated regularly, you stay in control. When it's vague or incomplete, the project controls you.

This chapter gives you a simple, practical system for building and managing a budget that works for any project, large or small.

5.1 Why Budgeting Matters

A well-built budget:

- Prevents surprises
- Reduces stress
- Improves decision-making
- Strengthens bidding accuracy
- Helps you prioritize

- Protects you from unnecessary costs
- Keeps the project aligned with your goals

A weak budget does the opposite. It creates confusion, invites assumptions, and forces you into reactive decisions.

Budgeting is not about predicting the future — it's about preparing for it.

5.2 The Three Components of a Strong Budget

Every construction budget has three essential components:

1. Base Costs — The known, measurable costs of labor, materials, and services
2. Allowances — Estimated costs for items not yet selected
3. Contingencies — Funds reserved for unknowns and unexpected conditions

When all three components are present and realistic, your budget becomes a powerful management

5.3 Base Costs: The Foundation of Your Budget

Base costs include:

- Demolition
- Structural work
- Mechanical, electrical, and plumbing systems
- Finishes and fixtures
- Labor and materials
- Equipment and rentals
- General conditions
- Contractor overhead and profit

These costs become clearer as your scope and design become more detailed.

Your role:

- Ensure the scope is complete
- Require detailed cost breakdowns
- Compare bids apples-to-apples
- Ask for clarifications in writing

Base costs should never be a single lump sum. Breakdowns create transparency.

5.4 Allowances: The Hidden Budget Trap

Allowances are placeholders for items not yet selected, such as:

- Appliances
- Fixtures
- Flooring
- Lighting
- Cabinets
- Hardware

Allowances are necessary — but dangerous if unrealistic.

To manage allowances effectively:

- Set realistic values based on your preferences
- Avoid low allowances designed to make bids appear cheaper
- Update allowances as selections are made
- Track allowance overages separately

Allowances are one of the most common sources of cost overruns. Manage them carefully.

5.5 Contingencies: Your Safety Net

Contingencies protect you from:

- Hidden conditions
- Design changes
- Permit requirements
- Material delays
- Unforeseen site issues

Recommended contingency levels:

- 10–20% for remodels (higher risk)
- 5–10% for new construction
- 15–25% for older buildings or unknown conditions

Contingencies are not "extra money." They are part of a responsible budget.

See "How Much Contingency Is Enough?" in the *Construction Management Made Easy First Edition ISBN 0-9668245-0-4

5.6 Soft Costs: The Often-Forgotten Budget Items

Soft costs include:

- Design fees
- Engineering fees

- Permit fees
- Surveys
- Inspections
- Testing
- Legal or consulting fees
- HOA or condo review fees

Owners often forget these costs — and they add up quickly.

Include them early to avoid surprises later.

5.7 Indirect Costs: The Costs You Don't See Coming

Indirect costs include:

- Temporary housing
- Storage
- Moving costs
- Lost rental income
- Business interruption
- Utility upgrades
- Temporary power or water

These costs are real and should be part of your planning.

5.8 Using the Magic Budget Calculator App

The Magic Budget Calculator helps you:

- Estimate costs early
- Compare scenarios
- Identify cost drivers
- Adjust scope to fit your budget
- Build a realistic financial plan

It is not a replacement for detailed bids — it is a tool for early decision-making.

See "Magic Budget Calculator" on Constructionplace.com

5.9 Aligning Your Budget with Your Scope

Your budget and scope must match. If they don't, one of them must change.

To align scope and budget:

- Prioritize must-haves vs. nice-to-haves

- Identify high-cost items early
- Adjust materials or finishes
- Phase the project if needed
- Use value engineering strategically

Never force a project into an unrealistic budget. Adjust early, not during construction.

5.10 Aligning Your Budget with Your Schedule

Schedule affects cost more than most owners realize.

Costs influenced by schedule include:

- Labor availability
- Material lead times
- Seasonal conditions
- Temporary housing
- Permit timelines
- Contractor workload

A rushed schedule increases costs. A realistic schedule saves money.

5.11 Tracking Your Budget Throughout the Project

A budget is a living document. Update it when:

- Design changes
- Scope evolves
- Allowances are selected
- Bids are received
- Change orders occur
- Contingency funds are used

Use tools such as:

- Budget worksheets
- Allowance trackers
- Payment logs
- Change order logs

Tracking prevents surprises and keeps you in control.

5.12 Understanding Contractor Pricing

Contractor pricing includes:

- Labor
- Materials
- Subcontractors
- Equipment
- General Conditions - The rules of the contract
- General Requirements - The contractor's jobsite obligations and the costs to manage the project.
- Overhead

General Conditions; General Requirements define the contractor's jobsite obligations and the costs to manage the project.

- Profit

Understanding these components helps you:

- Compare bids accurately
- Negotiate fairly
- Identify red flags
- Avoid hidden costs

Transparency is essential.

5.13 Avoiding Common Budgeting Mistakes

Mistake 1: Starting without a complete scope
Solution: Define scope before budgeting.

Mistake 2: Ignoring soft costs
Solution: Include all fees and services.

Mistake 3: Underestimating allowances
Solution: Use realistic values based on your preferences.

Mistake 4: Not including contingencies
Solution: Build in a safety net.

Mistake 5: Failing to track changes
Solution: Update the budget regularly.

Mistake 6: Accepting vague bids
Solution: Require detailed breakdowns.

5.14 A Realistic Budget Creates Confidence

When your budget is clear and complete:

- You make better decisions
- You avoid unnecessary costs
- You communicate with confidence
- You negotiate from strength
- You stay in control

Budgeting is not about perfection — it's about preparation. With the right tools and structure, budgeting becomes simple, predictable, and stress-free.

Chapter 6 — Scheduling for Real People

A construction schedule is more than a list of dates — it is the roadmap that guides your entire project. A good schedule keeps everyone aligned, prevents delays, and helps you make decisions at the right time. A weak or unrealistic schedule creates confusion, stress, and unnecessary costs.

You don't need to be a scheduling expert to manage your project effectively. You just need a clear, simple structure and the discipline to follow it. This chapter gives you exactly that.

6.1 Why Scheduling Matters

A well-planned schedule:

- Keeps the project organized
- Helps you anticipate decisions
- Prevents costly delays
- Improves coordination among trades
- Reduces stress and uncertainty
- Keeps the team accountable
- Protects your budget

A poor schedule leads to:

- Rushed decisions
- Idle labor
- Material delays
- Rework
- Change orders
- Frustration

Scheduling is not about predicting the future — it's about preparing for it.

6.2 The Three Levels of Scheduling

Every project benefits from three levels of scheduling:

1. Milestone Schedule — The big picture
2. Phase Schedule — The roadmap for each phase
3. Detailed Task Schedule — The contractor's day-to-day plan

You don't need to manage every detail. You just need to understand the milestones and ensure the contractor's detailed schedule aligns with your goals.

6.3 The Milestone Schedule

The milestone schedule is your high-level overview. It includes the major events that define the project.

Typical milestones include:

- Project definition complete
- Budget approved
- Design complete
- Permits submitted
- Permits approved
- Bidding complete
- Contract signed
- Construction start
- Rough-in inspections
- Final inspections
- Substantial completion
- Final completion

Milestones help you track progress without getting lost in the details.

6.4 The Phase Schedule

Each project phase has its own timeline. The phase schedule breaks the project into manageable segments.

Typical phases include:

- Concept & feasibility
- Planning & pre-construction
- Design & documentation
- Bidding & procurement

- Construction
- Closeout

Each phase has decisions, deliverables, and deadlines. You never move to the next phase until the current one is complete.

6.5 The Detailed Task Schedule

This is the contractor's responsibility. It includes:

- Daily or weekly tasks
- Trade sequencing
- Material deliveries
- Inspections
- Subcontractor coordination
- Crew assignments

You don't need to manage this schedule — but you do need to review it and ensure it aligns with your milestones and phase schedule.

6.6 Understanding the Critical Path

The critical path is the sequence of tasks that determines the project's overall duration. If any task on the critical path is delayed, the entire project is delayed.

Examples of critical path tasks:

- Structural work
- Rough plumbing
- Rough electrical
- Inspections
- Drywall
- Final finishes

Understanding the critical path helps you focus on what matters most.

6.7 Scheduling Tools You Should Use

You don't need complex software. Simple tools work best.

Essential scheduling tools include:

- Milestone Schedule Template
- Phase Schedule Worksheet
- Decision Deadline Tracker
- Inspection and Permit Timeline

- Weekly Progress Report Template

These tools help you stay organized and make timely decisions.

6.8 Permits and Inspections: The Hidden Schedule Drivers

Permits and inspections often take longer than expected. They can delay:

- Demolition
- Structural work
- Plumbing and electrical rough-ins
- Drywall
- Final completion

To avoid delays:

- Submit permits early
- Track inspection dates
- Confirm requirements in writing
- Build buffer time into your schedule

Permits and inspections are not optional — plan for them.

6.9 Material Lead Times: The Silent Schedule Killer

Many materials require long lead times, including:

- Cabinets
- Windows and doors
- Specialty fixtures
- Custom finishes
- Mechanical equipment

Order these items early to avoid delays. Your contractor should provide a long-lead item list at the start of the project.

6.10 Working in Occupied Spaces

If your project takes place in an occupied home or building, scheduling becomes even more important.

Consider:

- Noise restrictions
- Access limitations
- Safety requirements

- Temporary relocations
- Utility shutdowns
- Staging areas

Occupied projects require more coordination — and more patience.

6.11 Seasonal and Weather Considerations

Weather affects:

- Concrete work
- Roofing
- Exterior finishes
- Landscaping
- Material deliveries

Plan your schedule around seasonal conditions to avoid delays and cost increases.

6.12 How to Review a Contractor's Schedule

When reviewing a contractor's schedule, look for:

- Clear milestones
- Logical sequencing
- Realistic durations
- Long-lead items identified
- Inspection dates included
- Contingency time built in
- Coordination among trades

If the schedule seems too optimistic, it probably is.

6.13 Tracking Progress During Construction

Use simple tools to track progress:

- Weekly progress reports
- Updated schedules
- Site photos
- Meeting minutes
- Inspection logs

Tracking progress helps you identify issues early — when they are easier and cheaper to fix.

6.14 Managing Delays

Delays happen. What matters is how you respond.

When a delay occurs:

- Identify the cause
- Determine if it affects the critical path
- Assess cost and schedule impacts
- Document everything
- Require a recovery plan
- Adjust the schedule as needed

Delays are manageable when documented and addressed early.

6.15 Avoiding Common Scheduling Mistakes

Mistake 1: Starting construction too early
Solution: Complete planning and design first.

Mistake 2: Not ordering long-lead items early
Solution: Identify and order them at the start.

Mistake 3: Ignoring permit timelines
Solution: Submit early and track closely.

Mistake 4: Not reviewing the contractor's schedule
Solution: Require a detailed schedule before work begins.

Mistake 5: Failing to track progress
Solution: Use weekly updates and documentation.

6.16 A Realistic Schedule Creates Peace of Mind

When your schedule is clear and realistic:

- You make better decisions
- You avoid unnecessary delays
- You communicate with confidence
- You keep the team aligned
- You stay in control

Scheduling is not about perfection — it's about structure. With the right tools and approach, scheduling becomes simple, predictable, and stress-free.

Chapter 7 — Affordable Housing & Sustainable Practices

Construction today faces two urgent challenges: rising costs and the need for sustainable, energy-efficient buildings. Owners often feel forced to choose between affordability and sustainability, but the truth is that smart planning can achieve both. Affordable housing does not mean cutting corners, and sustainability does not mean overspending. When approached correctly, the two goals reinforce each other.

This chapter gives you practical strategies to reduce costs, improve efficiency, and build responsibly — without sacrificing quality or long-term performance.

7.1 Why Affordability and Sustainability Matter

Affordable, sustainable construction benefits:

- Owners — lower upfront costs and reduced long-term expenses
- Communities — safer, healthier, more resilient buildings
- The environment — reduced waste, energy use, and carbon footprint
- Future generations — buildings that last longer and cost less to maintain

Sustainability is not a trend — it is a practical approach to building smarter.

7.2 The Biggest Myths About Affordable and Sustainable Construction

Myth 1: Sustainable materials are always more expensive

Reality: Many sustainable options reduce long-term costs and often cost the same or less upfront.

Myth 2: Affordable housing means low quality

Reality: Quality comes from planning, not price.

Myth 3: Energy efficiency requires major upgrades

Reality: Small improvements often deliver the biggest returns.

Myth 4: Sustainability is only for large projects

Reality: Every project — even a small remodel — can benefit.

7.3 The Three Pillars of Affordable, Sustainable Construction

1. Smart Planning — Reduce waste and avoid rework
2. Efficient Systems — Lower operating costs
3. Durable Materials — Reduce maintenance and replacement costs

These pillars guide every decision you make.

7.4 Smart Planning: The Foundation of Affordability

Most cost savings come from planning, not materials.

Smart planning includes:

- Designing to standard dimensions
- Minimizing structural changes
- Reducing unnecessary complexity
- Coordinating trades early
- Avoiding last-minute decisions
- Using phased planning to prevent rework

A well-planned project is always more affordable.

7.5 Designing for Efficiency

Efficient design reduces both upfront and long-term costs.

Key strategies:

- Maximize natural light
- Improve insulation
- Use energy-efficient windows
- Optimize room layouts
- Reduce wasted space
- Plan for future needs

Efficiency is not about spending more — it's about designing smarter.

7.6 Energy-Efficient Systems That Save Money

Energy-efficient systems reduce operating costs for decades.

High-impact upgrades include:

- LED lighting
- High-efficiency HVAC systems
- Low-flow plumbing fixtures
- Smart thermostats
- Energy-efficient appliances
- Solar-ready electrical systems

These upgrades often pay for themselves quickly.

7.7 Water Efficiency and Plumbing Strategies

Water efficiency is essential for sustainability — and for lowering utility bills.

Effective strategies include:

- Low-flow fixtures
- Efficient water heaters
- Insulated hot water lines
- Leak detection systems
- Smart irrigation
- Coordinated plumbing replacements during remodels

Coordinating plumbing work with other upgrades saves significant time and money.

7.8 Material Choices That Balance Cost and Sustainability

Sustainable materials don't have to be expensive.

Cost-effective options include:

- Engineered lumber
- Recycled or reclaimed materials
- Low-VOC paints and finishes - Low-VOC paint is paint formulated with reduced levels of volatile organic compounds, which means it emits fewer harmful fumes, improves indoor air quality, and meets modern environmental standards.
- Durable flooring (vinyl plank, tile, engineered wood)
- Fiber-cement siding
- Recycled insulation products

Choose materials that last — durability is the most sustainable choice.

7.9 Reducing Waste During Construction

Waste is expensive. Reducing waste saves money and protects the environment.

Strategies include:

- Accurate material takeoffs
- Prefabricated components
- Reuse of existing materials
- Recycling construction debris
- Efficient demolition planning
- Clear staging and storage areas

Waste reduction is one of the easiest ways to improve affordability.

7.10 Affordable Housing Strategies for Owners and Communities

Affordable housing requires smart, scalable solutions.

Effective strategies include:

- Modular or prefabricated construction
- Standardized design templates
- Shared infrastructure
- Mixed-use planning
- Adaptive reuse of existing buildings
- Community-driven planning processes

These strategies reduce costs without reducing quality.

7.11 Incentives, Rebates, and Funding Opportunities

Many jurisdictions offer financial incentives for sustainable construction, including:

- Energy-efficiency rebates
- Solar incentives
- Water-saving rebates
- Tax credits
- Low-interest financing
- Grants for affordable housing

These programs can significantly reduce project costs.

7.12 Long-Term Savings: The Hidden Value of Sustainability

Sustainable buildings cost less to operate and maintain.

Long-term savings come from:

- Lower utility bills
- Fewer repairs
- Longer-lasting materials
- Reduced maintenance
- Higher resale value

Sustainability is an investment — not an expense.

7.13 Avoiding Common Mistakes in Affordable and Sustainable Construction

Mistake 1: Focusing only on upfront costs
Solution: Consider long-term operating costs.

Mistake 2: Choosing cheap materials that fail early

Solution: Prioritize durability.

Mistake 3: Ignoring energy efficiency

Solution: Invest in high-impact upgrades.

Mistake 4: Over-customizing the design

Solution: Use standard dimensions and components.

Mistake 5: Not coordinating plumbing and mechanical upgrades

Solution: Combine work to reduce labor and disruption.

7.14 Building a Better Future, One Project at a Time

Affordable, sustainable construction is not complicated. It is simply a matter of:

- Planning smart
- Choosing wisely
- Reducing waste
- Investing in efficiency
- Building for the long term

When owners lead with clarity and purpose, they create buildings that are affordable to build, affordable to maintain, and sustainable for generations.

Chapter 8 — Choosing the Right Delivery Method

One of the most important decisions you will make as an owner is selecting the right project delivery method. The delivery method determines how your project is designed, priced, managed, and built. It affects cost, schedule, quality, communication, and your level of control. Choosing the wrong method can lead to confusion, conflict, and unnecessary expense. Choosing the right one sets the stage for a smooth, predictable project.

This chapter explains the major delivery methods, their advantages and disadvantages, and how to choose the one that best fits your goals, budget, and risk tolerance.

8.1 What Is a Delivery Method?

A delivery method defines:

- Who designs the project
- Who builds the project
- How contracts are structured
- How pricing is determined
- How risk is allocated
- How communication flows

Delivery methods are not one-size-fits-all. The right choice depends on your project's complexity, timeline, budget, and your own experience as an owner.

8.2 The Four Most Common Delivery Methods

1. Design–Bid–Build (DBB)
2. Design–Build (DB)
3. Construction Management at Risk (CMAR)
4. Owner–Builder / Self-Managed

Each method has strengths and weaknesses. Understanding them helps you make an informed decision.

8.3 Design–Bid–Build (DBB)

The Traditional Method

Design–Bid–Build is the most widely used delivery method, especially for public projects.

How it works

1. You hire a designer to create complete plans and specifications.
2. Contractors bid on the completed design.
3. You select the lowest responsible bidder.
4. Construction begins under a separate contract.

Advantages

- Clear separation between design and construction
- Competitive bidding protects pricing
- Well-understood and widely used
- Strong owner control

Disadvantages

- Longer schedule (design must be complete before bidding)
- Designers may not fully understand construction costs
- Contractors may exploit design gaps
- Higher risk of change orders

Best for

- Projects with well-defined scope
- Owners who want competitive pricing
- Public or regulated projects

8.4 Design–Build (DB)

One Team, One Contract

Design–Build combines design and construction under a single contract.

How it works

1. You hire a design–build team.
2. They design and build the project as a unified group.
3. Pricing and design evolve together.

Advantages

- Faster delivery
- Single point of responsibility
- Fewer change orders
- Better coordination between design and construction

Disadvantages

- Less owner control over design details
- Harder to compare pricing
- Risk of “value engineering” that reduces quality
- Requires a highly trustworthy team

Best for

- Projects with tight schedules
- Owners who want simplicity
- Projects where design flexibility is acceptable

8.5 Construction Management at Risk (CMAR)

A Hybrid Approach

CMAR gives you a construction manager (CM) who acts as your advisor during design and your contractor during construction.

How it works

1. You hire a CM early in the design phase.
2. The CM provides cost estimates, scheduling, and constructability input.
3. The CM guarantees a maximum price (GMP).
4. Construction begins under the CM’s management.

Advantages

- Early cost and schedule input

- Reduced risk of surprises
- Better coordination
- GMP provides cost protection

Disadvantages

- Less competitive pricing
- CM may favor certain subcontractors
- Requires strong owner oversight

Best for

- Complex projects
- Projects with uncertain scope
- Owners who want early cost control

8.6 Owner–Builder / Self-Managed

Maximum Control, Maximum Responsibility
In this method, the owner acts as the general contractor.

How it works

1. You hire and manage subcontractors directly.
2. You coordinate scheduling, inspections, and payments.
3. You assume full responsibility for the project.

Advantages

- Maximum control
- Potential cost savings
- Direct oversight of quality

Disadvantages

- High risk
- Requires significant time and expertise
- Liability and insurance challenges
- Difficult for complex projects

Best for

- Small projects
- Experienced owners
- Projects with flexible schedules

8.7 How Delivery Methods Affect Cost

Delivery method influences:

- Pricing transparency
- Change order frequency
- Contractor markup
- Design quality
- Risk allocation

For example:

- DBB offers competitive pricing but more change orders.
- DB offers fewer change orders but less pricing transparency.
- CMAR offers early cost control but less competition.

Choose the method that aligns with your financial priorities.

8.8 How Delivery Methods Affect Schedule

If schedule is your top priority

- Design–Build (DB) is fastest
- CMAR is second fastest
- Design–Bid–Build is (DBB) is lowest
- Owner-Builder (OB) is not the fastest delivery method unless the owner is highly experienced, fully available, and able to make rapid decisions.

But speed should never come at the expense of clarity or quality.

8.9 How Delivery Methods Affect Risk

Risk shifts depending on the method:

- DBB - Owner holds most risk
- DB - Contractor holds more risk
- CMAR - Shared risk with GMP protection
- OB - Owner–Builder — Owner holds all risk

Understanding risk allocation helps you choose wisely.

8.10 How to Choose the Right Delivery Method

Ask yourself:

- How clearly is my project defined?
- How important is schedule?

- How important is competitive pricing?
- How much control do I want?
- How much risk am I willing to take?
- How experienced is my team?

Your answers will point you toward the right method.

8.11 Tools for Evaluating Delivery Methods

Use:

- Delivery Method Comparison Chart
- Risk Assessment Worksheet
- Budget Alignment Checklist
- Schedule Priority Worksheet
- Owner Experience Assessment

These tools help you make a confident, informed decision.

8.12 Avoiding Common Mistakes

Mistake 1: Choosing based on price alone
Solution: Consider risk, schedule, and control.

Mistake 2: Selecting a method before defining the project
Solution: Complete project definition first.

Mistake 3: Assuming one method fits all projects
Solution: Evaluate each project independently.

Mistake 4: Ignoring your own experience level
Solution: Choose a method that matches your comfort and capacity.

8.13 The Right Delivery Method Sets the Tone

When you choose the right delivery method:

- Costs become predictable
- Communication improves
- Risk decreases
- Quality increases
- The project runs smoothly

Delivery method is not just a contract choice — it is a strategic decision that shapes your entire project.

Chapter 9 — Hiring Designers, Contractors & Consultants

Hiring the right team is one of the most important decisions you will make as an owner. Even the best-planned project will fail if the people doing the work are unqualified, unorganized, or misaligned with your goals. Conversely, a strong team can overcome challenges, protect your budget, and deliver a high-quality project with minimal stress.

This chapter gives you a practical, step-by-step system for selecting designers, contractors, and consultants who will support your vision, communicate clearly, and perform with professionalism.

9.1 Why Hiring Matters More Than Anything Else

Your team determines:

- The quality of the design
- The accuracy of the budget
- The reliability of the schedule
- The number of change orders
- The level of communication
- The amount of stress you experience
- The long-term performance of your building

Hiring is not about choosing the cheapest or the most charismatic. It's about choosing the most qualified, trustworthy, and aligned with your goals.

9.2 The Three Qualities You Must Look For

Every designer, contractor, and consultant should demonstrate:

1. Competence

They must have the skills, experience, and technical knowledge to do the job.

2. Communication

They must respond promptly, explain clearly, and document consistently.

3. Character

They must be honest, transparent, and willing to collaborate.

If any one of these qualities is missing, the project will suffer.

PART I — HIRING DESIGNERS

9.3 The Role of the Designer

Designers:

- Translate your goals into drawings
- Coordinate engineering

- Ensure code compliance
- Influence cost and constructability
- Shape the look, feel, and function of your project

A good designer saves you money. A poor designer costs you money.

9.4 How to Find Qualified Designers

Sources include:

- Referrals from trusted professionals
- Professional associations
- Online portfolios
- Local building departments
- Past project owners

Look for designers with experience in your project type and building type.

9.5 Questions to Ask Designers

Ask:

- What similar projects have you completed?
- How do you manage cost control during design?
- How do you coordinate with engineers and contractors?
- What is your communication process?
- What is included in your fee — and what is not?
- How do you handle revisions?

Their answers reveal their professionalism and approach.

9.6 Red Flags When Hiring Designers

Avoid designers who:

- Are vague about fees
- Don't ask questions about your goals
- Push their own agenda
- Are slow to respond
- Have no recent or relevant experience
- Cannot explain the permitting process

If they are disorganized during the interview, they will be worse during the project.

PART II — HIRING CONTRACTORS

9.7 The Role of the Contractor

Contractors:

- Manage labor and subcontractors
- Coordinate scheduling
- Order materials
- Maintain safety
- Ensure quality
- Handle inspections
- Control the day-to-day work

A contractor is not just a builder — they are your project's operational leader.

9.8 How to Find Qualified Contractors

Sources include:

- Referrals
- Local building departments
- Trade associations
- Online reviews (with caution)
- Past project owners
- Your designer's recommendations

Always verify licenses, insurance, and bonding capacity.

9.9 The Interview Process

Ask contractors:

- What similar projects have you completed?
- Who will supervise the job?
- How many projects do you run at once?
- How do you handle scheduling and delays?
- How do you manage change orders?
- What is your communication process?
- Can you provide references — and can I visit a current job?

The interview is your chance to assess competence and character.

9.10 The Importance of Competitive Bidding

Competitive bidding:

- Protects you from inflated pricing
- Reveals assumptions and exclusions
- Helps you compare contractors fairly
- Encourages transparency

Even in design-build or negotiated contracts, you should still compare pricing.

9.11 How to Compare Bids

Compare:

- Scope of work
- Exclusions
- Allowances
- Unit prices
- Schedule
- Warranty terms
- Payment terms
- Contractor markup

Never choose a contractor based on price alone. Choose based on value.

9.12 Red Flags When Hiring Contractors

Avoid contractors who:

- Pressure you to sign quickly
- Offer vague or incomplete bids
- Refuse to provide references
- Lack proper insurance
- Have unresolved complaints
- Are unwilling to document decisions
- Avoid written communication

If something feels off, trust your instincts.

PART III — HIRING CONSULTANTS

9.13 Types of Consultants You May Need

Depending on your project, you may need:

- Structural engineers

- Mechanical, electrical, and plumbing (MEP) engineers
- Surveyors
- Geotechnical engineers
- Energy consultants
- Accessibility specialists
- Permit expediters
- Third-party inspectors

Consultants provide expertise that protects you from risk.

9.14 How to Evaluate Consultants

Look for:

- Relevant experience
- Clear communication
- Reasonable fees
- Strong references
- Ability to coordinate with your designer and contractor

Consultants should simplify your project — not complicate it.

9.15 When to Bring Consultants Onboard

Bring consultants in:

- Early enough to influence design
- Before major decisions are made
- Before bidding
- Before construction begins

Late involvement leads to redesigns and delays.

PART IV — MAKING THE FINAL DECISION

9.16 The Selection Matrix

Use a simple scoring system to compare candidates based on:

- Experience
- Communication
- Cost
- Schedule
- References

- Professionalism
- Compatibility

A structured approach prevents emotional or rushed decisions.

9.17 Checking References the Right Way

Ask past clients:

- Were they responsive?
- Did they stay on budget?
- Were there many change orders?
- Was the schedule realistic?
- How did they handle problems?
- Would you hire them again?

References reveal what interviews cannot.

9.18 Verifying Licenses, Insurance & Legal Standing

Always verify:

- Contractor license status
- Insurance coverage
- Bonding capacity
- Bonding rate
- Workers' compensation
- Litigation history
- Complaints or violations

This protects you from liability and financial risk.

9.19 Trust Your Instincts — But Verify Everything

If someone seems evasive, disorganized, or difficult during the hiring process, they will be worse during construction. Trust your instincts — but always verify with documentation.

9.20 Hiring the Right Team Sets the Stage for Success

When you hire the right people:

- Communication improves
- Costs stay under control
- Quality increases
- Delays decrease

- Stress disappears
- The project becomes predictable

Hiring is not a gamble — it is a structured process. With the right approach, you can build a team that supports your goals and delivers a successful project.

Chapter 10 — Contracts That Protect You

A construction contract is more than a legal document — it is the foundation of your project's success. A good contract creates clarity, sets expectations, and protects you from unnecessary risk. A weak contract invites misunderstandings, disputes, delays, and cost overruns.

Most owners sign contracts they don't fully understand. Contractors often use their own forms, written to protect their interests — not yours. This chapter gives you the knowledge and tools to negotiate fair, balanced, and protective agreements that support your goals and keep your project on track.

10.1 Why Contracts Matter

A strong contract:

- Defines the scope clearly
- Establishes responsibilities
- Sets the schedule
- Controls costs
- Reduces disputes
- Protects you from liability
- Ensures quality
- Provides recourse when things go wrong

A weak contract leaves everything open to interpretation — and interpretation is expensive.

10.2 The Essential Elements of a Construction Contract

Every construction contract should include:

1. Scope of Work
2. Schedule
3. Price and Payment Terms
4. Allowances and Contingencies
5. Change Order Procedures
6. Insurance and Bonding Requirements
7. Warranties
8. Dispute Resolution

9. Termination Rights
10. Closeout Requirements

If any of these elements are missing or vague, the contract is incomplete.

10.3 Scope of Work: The Heart of the Contract

The scope of work defines exactly what the contractor will do — and what they will not do.

A strong scope includes:

- Detailed descriptions of work
- Specific materials and finishes
- Drawings and specifications
- Exclusions and assumptions
- Responsibilities for permits and inspections

A vague scope leads to change orders, disputes, and inflated costs.

10.4 Schedule: Setting Expectations

The schedule should include:

- Start date
- Completion date
- Milestones
- Inspection dates
- Long-lead item deadlines
- Penalties or incentives (if applicable)

Avoid open-ended schedules such as "work will begin when permits are approved." Be specific.

10.5 Price and Payment Terms

There are three common pricing structures:

1. Lump Sum (Fixed Price)
Predictable cost, but requires complete design.

2. Cost-Plus
Flexible, but requires strong oversight.

3. Guaranteed Maximum Price (GMP)
Cost protection with flexibility.

Payment terms should include:

- Deposit limits
- Progress payment schedule
- Retainage (typically 5–10%)
- Conditions for final payment

Never pay too much upfront. Payments should follow progress — not promises.

10.6 Allowances and Contingencies

Allowances must be:

- Realistic
- Clearly defined
- Tracked separately

Contingencies must be:

- Appropriate for project type
- Used only for true unknowns
- Documented when spent

These items protect your budget — but only when managed properly.

10.7 Change Orders: Your Protection Against Surprise Costs

Change orders must be:

- Written
- Approved before work begins
- Priced clearly
- Documented with cost and schedule impacts

Verbal agreements lead to disputes. Written change orders protect everyone.

10.8 Insurance and Bonding Requirements

Your contractor should carry:

- General liability insurance
- Workers' compensation
- Auto liability
- Builder's risk (for larger projects)

For larger or riskier projects, require:

- Performance bond

- Payment bond

Insurance protects you from liability. Bonds protect you from contractor failure.

*See "To Bond or Not to Bond?" in the *Construction Management Made Easy First Edition ISBN 0-9668245-0-4*

10.9 Warranties: Protecting Your Investment

Warranties should cover:

- Workmanship
- Materials
- Systems (HVAC, plumbing, electrical)
- Manufacturer warranties

Typical warranty periods:

- 1 year for workmanship
- 2 years for mechanical systems
- 10 years for structural components

Make sure warranty terms are in writing — not verbal promises.

10.10 Dispute Resolution

Disputes happen. Your contract should specify how they will be resolved.

Options include:

- Negotiation
- Mediation
- Arbitration
- Litigation

Mediation is often the fastest and least expensive. Arbitration can be binding and costly. Litigation should be a last resort.

10.11 Termination Rights

Your contract should allow you to terminate:

- For cause (non-performance)
- For convenience (with notice)

Termination clauses protect you if the contractor fails to perform.

10.12 Closeout Requirements

Closeout should include:

- Punch list completion
- Final inspections
- As-built drawings
- O&M manuals
- Warranty documents
- Lien releases
- Final payment

A project is not complete until closeout is complete.

10.13 Red Flags in Construction Contracts

Avoid contracts that:

- Are handwritten or incomplete
- Lack detailed scope
- Require large upfront payments
- Exclude warranties
- Allow unilateral changes
- Limit your rights
- Shift unreasonable risk to you
- Are presented as "standard" but cannot be explained

If a contractor refuses to revise a contract, walk away.

10.14 Negotiating a Fair Contract

You don't need to be a lawyer to negotiate effectively. Use these principles:

- Be clear and direct
- Ask questions
- Require written documentation
- Remove vague language
- Protect your rights
- Align the contract with your goals

A fair contract protects both parties — not just the contractor.

10.15 Tools for Reviewing Contracts

Use:

- Contract Review Checklist
- Scope Verification Worksheet
- Payment Schedule Template
- Change Order Procedure Checklist
- Risk Allocation Worksheet

These tools help you identify gaps and protect your interests.

10.16 A Strong Contract Creates a Strong Project

When your contract is clear, complete, and fair:

- Costs stay predictable
- Communication improves
- Disputes decrease
- Quality increases
- Stress disappears
- The project becomes manageable

A strong contract is not about mistrust — it is about clarity. Clarity protects everyone.

Chapter 11 — Communication & Documentation

Construction projects succeed when communication is clear and documentation is consistent. They fail when assumptions replace facts, when decisions aren't recorded, and when information is scattered across emails, texts, and conversations. Most disputes, delays, and cost overruns can be traced back to poor communication and weak documentation.

This chapter gives you a simple, structured system for communicating effectively, documenting decisions, and keeping your project organized from start to finish. You don't need to be a construction expert — you just need a process.

11.1 Why Communication Matters

Clear communication:

- Prevents misunderstandings
- Reduces conflict
- Speeds up decision-making
- Keeps the team aligned
- Improves quality
- Protects your budget

- Builds trust

Poor communication leads to:

- Confusion
- Rework
- Delays
- Change orders
- Frustration
- Legal disputes

Communication is not optional — it is the foundation of project success.

11.2 Why Documentation Matters Even More

Documentation is your protection. If it's not written down, it didn't happen.

Good documentation:

- Clarifies expectations
- Records decisions
- Tracks progress
- Supports payments
- Protects you in disputes
- Creates accountability

Documentation is not about paperwork — it's about clarity.

PART I — COMMUNICATION

11.3 The Three Rules of Construction Communication

1. Be clear — Say exactly what you mean.
2. Be consistent — Use the same tools and formats throughout the project.
3. Be documented — Follow every conversation with written confirmation.

These rules prevent 90% of construction problems.

11.4 Communication Channels You Should Use

Use:

- Email for decisions and confirmations
- Scheduled meetings for coordination
- Written agendas and minutes
- Project logs and templates

- Constructionplace.com tools for centralized communication

Avoid:

- Verbal agreements
- Text messages for important decisions
- Unscheduled conversations that go undocumented

Professional communication protects you.

11.5 Weekly Progress Meetings

Weekly meetings keep the project on track.

A good meeting includes:

- Agenda
- Progress updates
- Schedule review
- Budget review
- Change order status
- Issues and resolutions
- Action items

Meetings should be short, structured, and documented.

11.6 Meeting Minutes: Your Most Powerful Tool

Meeting minutes should include:

- Date and attendees
- Topics discussed
- Decisions made
- Action items
- Deadlines
- Responsibilities

Minutes prevent “he said, she said” disputes and keep everyone accountable.

11.7 The Decision Log

A decision log tracks:

- What was decided
- Who decided it
- When it was decided

- Why it was decided
- Impacts on cost or schedule

This log prevents forgotten decisions and protects you from unauthorized changes.

11.8 The RFI (Request for Information) Process

RFIs clarify questions during construction.

A proper RFI includes:

- The question
- The location or drawing reference
- The proposed solution (optional)
- The required response date

RFIs should be answered quickly and documented clearly.

PART II — DOCUMENTATION

11.9 The Documentation System Every Owner Needs

Your documentation system should include:

- Contract documents
- Drawings and specifications
- Meeting minutes
- Decision logs
- Change order logs
- Budget and payment logs
- Inspection reports
- Submittals and approvals
- Photos and videos
- Closeout documents

Keep everything in one place — not scattered across devices.

11.10 Document Control Log

A document control log tracks:

- Document versions
- Revision dates
- Distribution lists
- Approvals

This prevents outdated drawings from being used in the field.

11.11 Submittals and Approvals

Submittals include:

- Shop drawings
- Product data
- Samples
- Mockups

You must review submittals to ensure they match your expectations and the contract requirements.

11.12 Daily Site Reports

Daily reports should include:

- Weather
- Crew size
- Work performed
- Deliveries
- Inspections
- Issues or delays

Daily reports help you track progress and identify problems early.

11.13 Photo Documentation

Photos provide:

- Visual proof of progress
- Evidence of hidden conditions
- Support for change orders
- Protection in disputes

Take photos regularly — especially before walls are closed.

11.14 Inspection Logs

Track:

- Required inspections
- Dates requested
- Dates completed
- Results

- Corrections required

Inspection delays are a major cause of schedule problems — stay ahead of them.

11.15 Change Order Documentation

Every change order should include:

- Description of the change
- Reason for the change
- Cost impact
- Schedule impact
- Supporting documentation
- Owner approval

Never approve a change order without full documentation.

11.16 Payment Documentation

Payment documentation should include:

- Progress payment applications
- Percentage of work completed
- Stored materials
- Lien releases
- Updated schedule
- Updated budget

Never pay for work that is not complete or documented.

PART III — STAYING ORGANIZED

11.17 Centralizing Your Information

Use a single system to store:

- Documents
- Photos
- Logs
- Reports
- Communications

Constructionplace.com provides a centralized platform designed specifically for owners.

11.18 Consistency Is More Important Than Complexity

You don't need complicated software. You just need:

- Simple tools
- Clear processes
- Consistent habits

Consistency prevents mistakes.

11.19 Avoiding Common Communication and Documentation Mistakes

Mistake 1: Relying on verbal agreements
Solution: Document everything.

Mistake 2: Not using meeting minutes
Solution: Record decisions and action items.

Mistake 3: Poor document organization
Solution: Centralize your files.

Mistake 4: Not tracking changes
Solution: Use a change order log.

Mistake 5: Failing to confirm decisions in writing
Solution: Send follow-up emails after discussions.

11.20 Communication and Documentation Create Control

When communication is clear and documentation is consistent:

- Problems are caught early
- Decisions are made confidently
- Costs stay predictable
- Schedules stay realistic
- Disputes are minimized
- Stress disappears

Communication and documentation are not extra work — they are the work that makes everything else easier.

Chapter 12 — Quality Control & Inspections

Quality doesn't happen by accident. It happens because the owner sets clear expectations, uses structured tools, and verifies the work at every stage. Most construction defects, warranty issues, and long-term maintenance problems can be traced back to poor quality control during construction. The good news is that owners don't need to be experts to ensure high-quality work — they just need a system.

This chapter gives you a practical, step-by-step approach to quality control and inspections that works for any project, large or small.

12.1 Why Quality Control Matters

Strong quality control:

- Prevents defects and rework
- Reduces long-term maintenance costs
- Improves safety
- Ensures compliance with codes and standards
- Protects your investment
- Reduces disputes and warranty claims

Weak quality control leads to:

- Hidden defects
- Water damage
- Structural issues
- Mechanical failures
- Costly repairs
- Frustration and finger-pointing

Quality is not something you "hope for." It is something you verify.

12.2 The Owner's Role in Quality Control

You don't need to inspect every nail or understand every technical detail. Your role is to:

- Set expectations
- Require documentation
- Use checklists
- Track inspections
- Ask questions
- Verify critical milestones
- Bring in experts when needed

Quality control is about leadership, not technical expertise.

PART I — SETTING EXPECTATIONS

12.3 Quality Starts with Clear Requirements

Quality begins long before construction starts. It begins with:

- A complete scope of work
- Detailed drawings and specifications
- Clear material selections
- Defined workmanship standards
- A strong contract

If expectations are vague, quality will be inconsistent.

12.4 Workmanship Standards

Workmanship standards define the level of quality you expect.

Standards may include:

- Industry best practices
- Manufacturer installation requirements
- Code requirements
- Tolerances for finishes
- Alignment, spacing, and leveling standards

Include workmanship standards in your contract and review them with your contractor.

12.5 Pre-Construction Meeting

Before construction begins, hold a pre-construction meeting to review:

- Scope
- Schedule
- Quality expectations
- Inspection requirements
- Communication procedures
- Safety protocols

This meeting sets the tone for the entire project.

PART II — INSPECTIONS

12.6 Types of Inspections

There are three types of inspections:

1. Code Inspections

Required by the building department.

2. Contractor Inspections

Performed by the contractor and subcontractors.

3. Owner or Third-Party Inspections

Performed by you or an independent inspector.

Each type plays a different role in ensuring quality.

12.7 Code Inspections: Minimum Standards

Code inspections verify:

- Structural integrity
- Electrical safety
- Plumbing compliance
- Mechanical systems
- Fire safety
- Energy efficiency

But remember: code is the minimum standard, not the quality standard.

Never rely solely on code inspections.

12.8 Contractor Inspections

Contractors should:

- Inspect their own work
- Verify subcontractor work
- Correct deficiencies before inspections
- Document progress
- Maintain quality control logs

If the contractor does not have a quality control process, that is a red flag.

12.9 Owner or Third-Party Inspections

Owners can hire:

- Home inspectors
- Specialty inspectors
- Structural engineers
- Mechanical or electrical experts
- Waterproofing specialists

Third-party inspections provide independent verification and protect you from hidden defects.

PART III — CRITICAL INSPECTION MILESTONES

12.10 Pre-Construction Walkthrough

Document:

- Existing conditions
- Potential risks
- Areas requiring protection
- Access and staging areas

Photos are essential.

12.11 Foundation and Structural Inspections

Verify:

- Footings
- Reinforcement
- Framing
- Shear walls
- Structural connections

Structural issues are expensive to fix later.

12.12 Rough-In Inspections

Before walls are closed, inspect:

- Plumbing
- Electrical
- HVAC
- Fire sprinklers
- Insulation
- Waterproofing

This is your last chance to catch hidden problems.

12.13 Waterproofing and Envelope Inspections

Water intrusion is the number one cause of building failure.

Inspect:

- Flashing
- Roofing
- Windows and doors
- Sealants
- Weather barriers

- Drainage systems

Bring in a specialist if needed.

12.14 Pre-Drywall Inspection

Before drywall goes up, verify:

- Framing alignment
- Blocking
- Insulation
- Mechanical and electrical placement
- Fire stopping

Once drywall is installed, hidden issues become expensive.

12.15 Finish Inspections

Inspect:

- Flooring
- Cabinets
- Trim
- Paint
- Tile
- Fixtures

Use a finish checklist to ensure consistency.

12.16 Final Inspection and Punch List

The punch list includes:

- Incomplete work
- Defects
- Adjustments
- Touch-ups
- Corrections

Do not release final payment until the punch list is complete.

PART IV — DOCUMENTING QUALITY

12.17 Inspection Logs

Track:

- Inspection dates

- Results
- Corrections required
- Follow-up inspections
- Responsible parties

Logs create accountability.

12.18 Photo Documentation

Take photos:

- Before work begins
- During critical stages
- Before walls are closed
- At completion

Photos protect you from disputes and support warranty claims.

12.19 Quality Control Checklists

Use checklists for:

- Structural work
- Plumbing
- Electrical
- HVAC
- Waterproofing
- Finishes

Checklists ensure nothing is overlooked.

12.20 Correcting Deficiencies

When deficiencies are found:

- Document them
- Notify the contractor in writing
- Set deadlines for correction
- Verify corrections
- Update logs

Never accept incomplete or substandard work.

PART V — AVOIDING COMMON QUALITY CONTROL MISTAKES

Mistake 1: Relying only on code inspections

Solution: Use your own inspections and checklists.

Mistake 2: Not inspecting before walls are closed

Solution: Conduct thorough rough-in and pre-drywall inspections.

Mistake 3: Not documenting deficiencies

Solution: Use logs, photos, and written notices.

Mistake 4: Accepting verbal assurances

Solution: Require written confirmation.

Mistake 5: Rushing the punch list

Solution: Take your time — this is your final protection.

12.21 Quality Control Protects Your Investment

When you use a structured quality control system:

- Defects are caught early
- Costs stay predictable
- Work meets your expectations
- Inspections run smoothly
- Disputes are minimized
- Your building performs better for years to come

Quality control is not extra work — it is the work that protects everything you've invested in your project.

Chapter 13 — Managing Changes, Delays & Disputes

Even the best-planned construction projects encounter changes, delays, and disagreements. These challenges are not signs of failure — they are normal parts of the process. What matters is how you manage them. Owners who use a structured system stay in control, protect their budget, and keep the project moving. Owners who react emotionally or rely on verbal agreements often face unnecessary costs, stress, and conflict.

This chapter gives you a clear, practical approach to managing changes, delays, and disputes with confidence and professionalism.

PART I — MANAGING CHANGES

13.1 Why Changes Happen

Changes occur for three reasons:

1. Owner-initiated changes

New ideas, upgrades, or scope adjustments.

2. Unforeseen conditions

Hidden issues discovered during construction.

3. Design or coordination issues

Missing details, conflicts, or errors in the drawings.

Changes are normal — but they must be managed properly.

13.2 The Golden Rule: No Verbal Change Orders

Never approve changes verbally.

Never authorize work without documentation.

Never rely on memory.

If it's not written down, it didn't happen.

13.3 The Change Order Process

A proper change order includes:

- Description of the change
- Reason for the change
- Cost impact
- Schedule impact
- Supporting documentation
- Owner approval before work begins

This protects you from surprise costs and disputes.

13.4 Pricing Change Orders

Change orders should be priced using:

- Labor rates
- Material costs
- Equipment costs
- Subcontractor quotes
- Contractor markup (as defined in the contract)

Require transparency. Ask for breakdowns — not lump sums.

13.5 Evaluating Change Orders

Before approving a change order, ask:

- Is this change necessary?
- Does it align with my goals?
- Is the price reasonable?
- Does it affect the schedule?
- Does it create future risks?

Make decisions based on facts — not pressure.

13.6 Tracking Change Orders

Use a Change Order Log to track:

- Pending changes
- Approved changes
- Rejected changes
- Cost impacts
- Schedule impacts

This keeps your budget and schedule under control.

PART II — MANAGING DELAYS

13.7 Why Delays Happen

Delays occur for many reasons, including:

- Weather
- Material shortages
- Long-lead items
- Inspection delays
- Design changes
- Labor shortages
- Coordination issues
- Unforeseen conditions

Delays are normal — but they must be documented and addressed early.

13.8 The Critical Path: What Really Matters

Not all delays affect the project completion date.

Only delays on the critical path extend the schedule.

Understanding the critical path helps you:

- Prioritize issues
- Avoid unnecessary panic
- Focus on what truly impacts completion

13.9 Documenting Delays

When a delay occurs, document:

- Date and time
- Cause of delay
- Impact on work
- Impact on schedule
- Responsible party
- Proposed recovery plan

Documentation prevents disputes later.

13.10 Delay Notices

Contractors must provide written delay notices that include:

- Reason for delay
- Duration of delay
- Impact on critical path
- Proposed mitigation

If they don't provide notice, they may lose the right to claim extra time or money.

13.11 Recovery Plans

A recovery plan outlines:

- How the contractor will regain lost time
- Additional labor or shifts
- Resequencing of work
- Acceleration strategies

A delay without a recovery plan is unacceptable.

13.12 Avoiding Common Delay Mistakes

Mistake 1: Accepting excuses without documentation
Solution: Require written delay notices.

Mistake 2: Not understanding the critical path
Solution: Review the schedule regularly.

Mistake 3: Allowing delays to accumulate
Solution: Require recovery plans immediately.

PART III — MANAGING DISPUTES

13.13 Why Disputes Happen

Disputes typically arise from:

- Miscommunication
- Unclear scope
- Poor documentation
- Unapproved changes
- Payment issues
- Quality concerns
- Schedule disagreements

Most disputes are preventable with strong communication and documentation.

13.14 The Owner's Approach to Disputes

Your approach should be:

- Calm
- Professional
- Fact-based
- Documented
- Solution-oriented

Never argue emotionally. Never escalate prematurely.

13.15 The Dispute Resolution Ladder

Use this step-by-step approach:

Step 1: Direct Discussion
Clarify the issue with the contractor.

Step 2: Written Documentation
Summarize the issue and your position.

Step 3: Meeting With Key Decision-Makers
Bring in the superintendent, project manager, or owner.

Step 4: Mediation
A neutral third party helps resolve the issue.

Step 5: Arbitration or Litigation

Last resort — expensive and time-consuming.

Most disputes are resolved in Steps 1–3.

13.16 Using Documentation to Resolve Disputes

Your best tools are:

- Meeting minutes
- Emails
- Photos
- Logs
- Schedules
- Contracts
- Change orders

Facts win disputes — not opinions.

13.17 Payment Disputes

Payment disputes often arise when:

- Work is incomplete
- Work is defective
- Documentation is missing
- Change orders are unclear
- Schedule is behind

Protect yourself by:

- Requiring lien releases
- Verifying work before payment
- Using retainage
- Documenting deficiencies

Never pay for work that is not complete.

13.18 Quality Disputes

Quality disputes occur when:

- Work does not meet standards
- Materials differ from specifications
- Workmanship is poor

Use:

- Workmanship standards
- Inspection reports
- Photos
- Third-party inspectors

Quality is not negotiable.

13.19 Avoiding Common Dispute Mistakes

Mistake 1: Relying on verbal agreements
Solution: Document everything.

Mistake 2: Getting emotional
Solution: Stay professional and fact-based.

Mistake 3: Ignoring small issues
Solution: Address problems early.

Mistake 4: Not using the contract
Solution: Refer to the contract for every dispute.

13.20 Structure Creates Control

When you manage changes, delays, and disputes with structure:

- Costs stay predictable
- Schedules stay realistic
- Quality improves
- Stress decreases
- Relationships stay professional
- The project stays on track

Construction is not about avoiding problems — it's about managing them effectively. With the right tools and approach, you can handle any challenge with confidence.

Chapter 14 — Plumbing, Electrical & Mechanical Essentials

Most owners feel intimidated by plumbing, electrical, and mechanical (PEM) systems — and for good reason. These systems are hidden behind walls, governed by strict codes, and essential to the safety, comfort, and long-term performance of any building. When they fail, the consequences are expensive, disruptive, and sometimes dangerous.

The good news is that owners don't need to be engineers or tradespeople to manage these systems effectively. You simply need to understand the basics, ask the right questions, and coordinate work strategically. This chapter gives you a clear, practical overview of the systems that matter most — and how to manage them with confidence.

PART I — PLUMBING ESSENTIALS

14.1 Why Plumbing Matters

Plumbing failures are among the most common — and most expensive — problems in buildings. Issues include:

- Leaks
- Corrosion
- Clogged drains
- Water damage
- Mold
- Flooding
- Insurance claims

Plumbing problems escalate quickly and often require invasive repairs. Prevention is far cheaper than reaction.

14.2 Supply vs. Drain Systems

Plumbing has two major components:

1. Supply Lines

Carry pressurized water into the building.

Failures can cause major flooding.

2. Drain, Waste & Vent (DWV) Lines

Carry wastewater out.

Failures cause backups, odors, and sanitation issues.

Each system has different risks and maintenance needs.

14.3 Common Pipe Materials

Copper

Durable but vulnerable to corrosion and pinhole leaks.

PEX

PEX is a flexible, affordable, durable, and corrosion-resistant plastic piping material used for water supply systems.

Cast Iron (DWV)

DWV stands for Drain, Waste, and Vent, the plumbing system that removes wastewater and sewer gases from a building and provides venting to maintain proper pressure and flow. Strong but prone to rust and cracking over time.

PVC / ABS

Common for modern DWV systems; affordable and durable. PVC and ABS are lightweight, durable, and affordable plastic piping materials commonly used in modern DWV (Drain, Waste, and Vent) systems. They resist corrosion, are easy to install, and provide long-lasting performance for residential and commercial plumbing applications.

PVC is quieter and more flexible, ideal for interior DWV.

ABS is stronger and more impact-resistant, ideal for underground or cold-weather use.

Understanding your building's pipe materials helps you anticipate future issues.

14.4 Signs of Plumbing Problems

Watch for:

- Discolored water
- Low pressure
- Stains on ceilings or walls
- Mold or mildew
- Unusual odors
- Noisy pipes
- Slow drains

Early detection prevents major damage.

14.5 Coordinating Plumbing Replacements During Remodels

This is one of the most important cost-saving strategies in the entire book.

When walls are open:

- Replace old pipes
- Upgrade valves
- Add shut-offs
- Improve insulation
- Correct code issues

Coordinating plumbing work during remodels saves:

- Time
- Money
- Future disruption
- Emergency repair costs

Owners who skip this step often regret it later.

14.6 Water Heaters & Efficiency

Types include:

- Tank
- Tankless
- Heat pump
- Solar-assisted

Key considerations:

- Capacity
- Recovery rate
- Energy efficiency
- Venting
- Location

A properly sized, efficient water heater reduces utility costs and improves comfort.

PART II — ELECTRICAL ESSENTIALS

14.7 Why Electrical Systems Matter

Electrical systems affect:

- Safety
- Lighting
- Appliances
- HVAC
- Technology
- Energy efficiency

Electrical failures can cause fires, outages, and equipment damage.

14.8 Electrical Panels & Capacity

Your electrical panel must:

- Have adequate capacity
- Be properly labeled
- Meet current code
- Support modern loads

Older buildings often require panel upgrades to support:

- Air conditioning
- EV chargers
- Induction ranges

- Modern electronics

Never overload an outdated system.

14.9 Wiring Types

Common wiring includes:

- Copper (modern standard)
- Aluminum (older, higher risk)
- Knob-and-tube (very old, unsafe)

If your building has outdated wiring, plan for upgrades.

14.10 GFCI & AFCI Protection

GFCI protection (Ground-Fault Circuit Interrupter) is a safety device that shuts off electrical power when it detects a ground fault, such as electricity flowing through water or a person. It prevents electrical shock and is required in wet or damp locations like kitchens, bathrooms, garages, and outdoor areas.

AFCI protection (Arc-Fault Circuit Interrupter) is a safety device that detects dangerous electrical arcing caused by damaged wires, loose connections, or faulty cords, and automatically shuts off the circuit. It prevents electrical fires and is required in most living areas of modern buildings.

These devices prevent:

- Shock
- Fire
- Electrical hazards

They are required in:

- Kitchens
- Bathrooms
- Outdoors
- Garages
- Bedrooms (AFCI)

Upgrading protection improves safety dramatically.

14.11 Lighting & Energy Efficiency

LED lighting offers:

- Lower energy use
- Longer lifespan
- Better quality

- Reduced heat

Lighting upgrades are one of the easiest ways to improve efficiency.

PART III — MECHANICAL (HVAC) ESSENTIALS

14.12 Why Mechanical Systems Matter

HVAC systems affect:

- Comfort
- Air quality
- Energy use
- Noise levels
- Maintenance costs

Mechanical systems are often the largest energy consumers in a building.

14.13 Types of HVAC Systems

Common systems include:

- Split systems
- Packaged units
- Heat pumps
- Mini-splits
- VRF/VRV systems

  VRF (Variable Refrigerant Flow) systems are high-efficiency HVAC systems that use refrigerant as the heating and cooling medium and vary the flow to multiple indoor units based on demand. They provide precise temperature control, energy savings, and simultaneous heating and cooling in different zones.

  VRV (Variable Refrigerant Volume) systems are the same technology as VRF, branded by Daikin. They use variable refrigerant volume to serve multiple zones with individualized control, offering high efficiency, flexible installation, and advanced heat-recovery capabilities.

- Central chilled water systems (large buildings)

Choose systems based on climate, building type, and efficiency goals.

14.14 Air Quality & Ventilation

Good ventilation:

- Reduces odors
- Controls humidity

- Prevents mold
- Improves health

Mechanical ventilation is essential in modern, airtight buildings.

14.15 Maintenance Requirements

HVAC systems require:

- Filter changes
- Coil cleaning
- Refrigerant checks
- Duct inspections
- Annual servicing

Neglected systems fail early and cost more to operate.

PART IV — COORDINATION & SAFETY

14.16 Why Coordination Matters

Plumbing, electrical, and mechanical systems overlap. Poor coordination leads to:

- Conflicts
- Rework
- Delays
- Code violations
- Increased costs

Coordination should occur during:

- Design
- Pre-construction
- Rough-in
- Inspections

A coordinated team prevents expensive mistakes.

14.17 Safety Considerations

Safety risks include:

- Electrical shock
- Gas leaks
- Carbon monoxide
- Water damage

- Fire hazards

Owners must ensure:

- Proper permits
- Licensed trades
- Inspections
- Code compliance

Safety is non-negotiable.

PART V — OWNER TOOLS & CHECKLISTS

14.18 Questions to Ask Your Plumber

- What is the condition of my pipes?
- Should I replace pipes during this remodel?
- Are there code issues I need to address?
- What materials do you recommend and why?

14.19 Questions to Ask Your Electrician

- Is my panel adequate?
- Do I need new circuits?
- Are there safety issues?
- What efficiency upgrades make sense?

14.20 Questions to Ask Your HVAC Contractor

- Is my system properly sized?
- How efficient is it?
- What maintenance is required?
- Are there air quality concerns?

14.21 PEM Systems Are the Heart of Your Building

When you understand and manage plumbing, electrical, and mechanical systems:

- Your building becomes safer
- Your utility costs decrease
- Your comfort improves
- Your maintenance costs drop
- Your property value increases
- Your risk of emergencies declines

You don't need to be an expert — you just need a system. This chapter gives you that system.

Chapter 15 — Remodeling, Repairs & Emergency Projects

Remodels, repairs, and emergency projects are some of the most challenging situations an owner will face. Unlike planned construction, these projects often involve tight timelines, limited access, unknown conditions, and emotional pressure. Decisions must be made quickly — but not carelessly. Costs can escalate rapidly if the owner does not stay in control.

This chapter gives you a clear, practical system for managing remodels, repairs, and emergencies with confidence. Whether you're upgrading a kitchen, repairing storm damage, or responding to a burst pipe at midnight, the principles remain the same: stay calm, stay organized, and follow a structured process.

PART I — REMODELING PROJECTS

15.1 Why Remodels Are More Complex Than New Construction

Remodels involve:

- Existing conditions
- Hidden problems
- Occupied spaces
- Limited access
- Noise and dust control
- Temporary utilities
- Coordination with residents or tenants

Remodels require more planning, not less.

15.2 The Importance of Pre-Remodel Investigations

Before starting a remodel, investigate:

- Plumbing conditions
- Electrical capacity
- Structural limitations
- Mechanical systems
- Moisture issues
- Code compliance
- Previous modifications

These investigations prevent surprises and reduce change orders.

15.3 Coordinating System Upgrades During Remodels

When walls are open, it is the perfect time to:

- Replace old pipes
- Upgrade wiring
- Add circuits
- Improve insulation
- Install shut-off valves
- Correct code issues

Coordinating upgrades during remodels saves enormous time and money later.

15.4 Working in Occupied Spaces

Occupied remodels require:

- Clear communication
- Dust control
- Noise management
- Temporary access routes
- Safety barriers
- Daily cleanup
- Respect for residents

A well-managed occupied remodel minimizes disruption and maintains trust.

15.5 Phasing Remodels to Reduce Disruption

Phasing strategies include:

- Working on one area at a time
- Scheduling noisy work during limited hours
- Providing temporary kitchens or bathrooms
- Relocating residents temporarily

Phasing reduces stress and keeps the project moving.

PART II — REPAIRS

15.6 Why Repairs Are Often More Expensive Than Planned Work

Repairs involve:

- Emergency labor rates
- Limited contractor availability
- Unknown conditions

- Damage containment
- Insurance coordination
- Temporary fixes

Repairs are reactive — but you can still manage them strategically.

15.7 Diagnosing the Problem Before Acting

Before authorizing repairs:

- Identify the root cause
- Document the damage
- Take photos and videos
- Shut off utilities if needed
- Prevent further damage

A rushed repair often leads to incomplete or incorrect solutions.

15.8 Getting Multiple Opinions

For non-emergency repairs:

- Get at least two opinions
- Compare scopes
- Ask for explanations
- Request written estimates

Different contractors may propose different solutions — choose the one that addresses the root cause, not just the symptoms.

15.9 Insurance Claims & Documentation

For insurance-related repairs:

- Document everything
- Notify your insurer immediately
- Keep receipts
- Save damaged materials for inspection
- Follow the insurer's process

Insurance companies require thorough documentation — be prepared.

15.10 Preventing Future Repairs

After repairs are complete:

- Identify contributing factors
- Address underlying issues

- Improve maintenance practices
- Upgrade outdated systems

Repairs are opportunities to prevent future problems.

PART III — EMERGENCY PROJECTS

15.11 What Counts as an Emergency?

Emergencies include:

- Burst pipes
- Electrical failures
- Gas leaks
- Roof leaks
- Flooding
- Fire damage
- Structural failures

Emergencies require immediate action — but not panic.

15.12 The Owner's Emergency Response Plan

Every owner should have:

- Emergency shut-off locations
- Contact information for key contractors
- Insurance policy details
- A communication plan
- A temporary relocation plan (if needed)

Preparation reduces damage and stress.

15.13 The First Hour: What to Do Immediately

1. Ensure safety

Evacuate if necessary.

2. Shut off utilities

Water, electricity, or gas.

3. Stop the damage

Contain leaks, cover openings, secure the area.

4. Document everything

Photos, videos, written notes.

5. Contact the right professionals

Plumber, electrician, roofer, restoration company.

6. Notify your insurer

Early notification speeds up claims.

15.14 Choosing Emergency Contractors

Emergency contractors should be:

- Licensed
- Insured
- Experienced
- Responsive
- Transparent

Avoid contractors who:

- Pressure you
- Demand large upfront payments
- Offer vague explanations
- Refuse to provide documentation

Emergencies attract opportunists — stay vigilant.

15.15 Temporary vs. Permanent Repairs

Temporary repairs:

- Stop damage
- Protect the building
- Allow time for proper planning

Permanent repairs:

- Address root causes
- Restore full function
- Meet code requirements

Never confuse a temporary fix with a permanent solution.

PART IV — COST CONTROL IN REMODELS, REPAIRS & EMERGENCIES

15.16 Why Costs Escalate

Costs increase when:

- Decisions are rushed
- Scope is unclear
- Contractors exploit urgency
- Documentation is weak
- Work is not coordinated

Structure prevents cost escalation.

15.17 Tools for Cost Control

Use:

- Emergency repair logs
- Change order logs
- Budget worksheets
- Photo documentation
- Written approvals

These tools keep you in control even under pressure.

15.18 Avoiding Common Mistakes

Mistake 1: Hiring the first contractor who answers the phone
Solution: Verify qualifications, even in emergencies.

Mistake 2: Approving work without documentation
Solution: Require written scopes and prices.

Mistake 3: Ignoring underlying issues
Solution: Fix root causes, not symptoms.

Mistake 4: Failing to coordinate system upgrades
Solution: Use remodels as opportunities to modernize.

Mistake 5: Not documenting damage for insurance
Solution: Take photos and videos immediately.

15.19 You Can Manage Any Remodel, Repair, or Emergency

When you use a structured approach:

- Emergencies become manageable
- Repairs become opportunities
- Remodels become predictable
- Costs stay under control

- Stress decreases
- Your building becomes safer and more reliable

You don't need to be a contractor — you just need a system. This chapter gives you that system.

Chapter 16 — Punch Lists, Final Payments & Warranties

The end of a construction project is where owners are most vulnerable. Everyone is tired, the contractor wants to finish, and the owner wants their space back. This is when details get missed, quality slips, and pressure builds to release final payment before the work is truly complete.

Finishing strong requires discipline. The punch list, final payment process, and warranty period are your last opportunities to ensure the project meets your expectations and contractual requirements. This chapter gives you a clear, structured system to protect your investment and close out your project with confidence.

PART I — THE PUNCH LIST

16.1 What Is a Punch List?

A punch list is a detailed list of:

- Incomplete work
- Defects
- Adjustments
- Touch-ups
- Corrections

It is created near the end of the project, but before final payment.

16.2 When to Create the Punch List

The punch list should be created when:

- The project is substantially complete
- Systems are operational
- Finishes are installed
- The space is usable

Do not create a punch list too early — or too late.

16.3 Who Creates the Punch List?

The punch list should involve:

- The owner
- The contractor
- The designer (if applicable)

- Third-party inspectors (optional but valuable)

Multiple perspectives ensure nothing is overlooked.

16.4 How to Conduct a Punch List Walkthrough

During the walkthrough:

- Bring a checklist
- Take photos
- Test all systems
- Check alignment and finishes
- Verify cleanliness
- Document everything

Move slowly and methodically. This is your final quality check.

16.5 What to Include in a Punch List

Include:

- Paint touch-ups
- Cabinet adjustments
- Door alignment
- Fixture installation issues
- Electrical outlet testing
- Plumbing leaks
- HVAC performance
- Flooring defects
- Hardware adjustments
- Missing items

If it's not perfect, it goes on the list.

16.6 Tracking Punch List Completion

Use a Punch List Log to track:

- Items
- Responsible party
- Status
- Completion dates
- Verification

Do not rely on verbal updates.

16.7 The Golden Rule: No Final Payment Until Punch List Completion

Final payment should only be released when:

- All punch list items are complete
- All inspections are passed
- All documentation is delivered
- All warranties are provided
- All lien releases are submitted

Final payment is your leverage — use it wisely.

PART II — FINAL PAYMENTS

16.8 What Final Payment Includes

Final payment typically includes:

- Remaining contract balance
- Release of retainage
- Payment for approved change orders
- Final adjustments

This is the last major financial transaction of the project.

16.9 Conditions for Final Payment

Before releasing final payment, require:

- Completed punch list
- Final inspection approval
- As-built drawings
- O&M manuals
- Warranty documents
- Lien releases
- Updated schedule
- Updated budget

If anything is missing, final payment should not be released.

16.10 Lien Releases: Your Legal Protection

Lien releases protect you from:

- Subcontractor claims
- Supplier claims
- Future disputes

Require lien releases:

- With every progress payment
- With final payment
- From all subcontractors and suppliers

Never skip this step.

16.11 Retainage: Your Final Leverage

Retainage (typically 5–10%) is withheld until:

- All work is complete
- All documentation is delivered
- All punch list items are resolved
- All punch list items have been completed and accepted

Retainage protects you from incomplete or rushed work.

16.12 Avoiding Common Final Payment Mistakes

Mistake 1: Paying too early
Solution: Require full completion and documentation.

Mistake 2: Accepting verbal assurances
Solution: Require written confirmation.

Mistake 3: Not verifying work personally
Solution: Conduct your own walkthrough.

Mistake 4: Forgetting lien releases
Solution: Make them mandatory.

PART III — WARRANTIES

16.13 Understanding Warranties

Warranties cover:

- Workmanship
- Materials
- Systems
- Manufacturer components

They protect you from defects that appear after completion.

16.14 Typical Warranty Periods

- 1 year — General workmanship
- 2 years — Mechanical, electrical, plumbing systems
- 10 years — Structural components
- Manufacturer warranties — Vary by product

Know what is covered — and what is not.

16.15 Warranty Documentation

Warranty documentation should include:

- Warranty terms
- Coverage periods
- Contact information
- Maintenance requirements
- Registration instructions

Keep all documents organized and accessible.

16.16 Warranty Tracking System

Use a Warranty Log to track:

- Start and end dates
- Covered items
- Contractor responsibilities
- Manufacturer contacts
- Service history

This ensures timely claims and proper maintenance.

16.17 Making Warranty Claims

When a problem arises:

- Document the issue
- Take photos
- Notify the contractor in writing
- Follow up regularly
- Track response times

Warranties are only useful if you enforce them.

16.18 Preventing Warranty Disputes

Prevent disputes by:

- Maintaining documentation
- Following maintenance requirements
- Reporting issues promptly
- Keeping communication in writing

Most disputes arise from poor documentation — not bad workmanship.

PART IV — PROJECT CLOSEOUT

16.19 Closeout Documents You Must Receive

Closeout should include:

- As-built drawings
- O&M manuals
- Warranty documents
- Final inspection reports
- Lien releases
- Final schedule
- Final budget
- Maintenance recommendations

Do not close the project without these documents.

16.20 Finishing Strong Protects Your Investment

When you finish strong:

- Quality is verified
- Costs are controlled
- Documentation is complete
- Warranties are enforceable
- Disputes are minimized
- Your building performs better
- Your stress disappears

The end of the project is not the time to relax — it is the time to be thorough. With the right structure, you can close out your project confidently and protect your investment for years to come.

Chapter 17 — Maintenance, Operations & Long-Term Planning

Construction doesn't end when the contractor leaves. In many ways, it's just beginning. A building is a living system — it ages, it wears, it responds to weather, use, and time. Owners who maintain their buildings proactively enjoy lower costs, fewer emergencies, and higher property values. Owners who neglect maintenance face breakdowns, insurance claims, special assessments, and expensive surprises.

This chapter gives you a clear, practical system for maintaining your building, managing operations, and planning for long-term needs. Whether you own a single home, a commercial property, or a condo unit in a large building, the principles remain the same: protect your investment, plan ahead, and stay organized.

PART I — MAINTENANCE

17.1 Why Maintenance Matters

Proactive maintenance:

- Extends the life of systems
- Reduces repair costs
- Prevents emergencies
- Improves safety
- Protects property value
- Reduces insurance claims
- Ensures comfort and reliability

Maintenance is not an expense — it is an investment.

17.2 The Three Types of Maintenance

1. Preventive Maintenance

Scheduled tasks that prevent breakdowns.

2. Predictive Maintenance

Monitoring systems to anticipate failures.

3. Corrective Maintenance

Fixing issues when they occur.

A strong maintenance program uses all three.

17.3 Creating a Maintenance Plan

A maintenance plan should include:

- Inventory of all systems
- Manufacturer recommendations
- Seasonal tasks

- Annual inspections
- Replacement timelines
- Budget estimates

A written plan keeps you organized and accountable.

17.4 Seasonal Maintenance Tasks

Spring

- Inspect roofing
- Clean gutters
- Test irrigation
- Service HVAC cooling

Summer

- Inspect exterior finishes
- Check plumbing insulation
- Review ventilation systems

Fall

- Service heating systems
- Clean drains
- Inspect weatherproofing

Winter

- Monitor pipes
- Check insulation
- Test smoke and CO detectors

Seasonal maintenance prevents seasonal emergencies.

17.5 System-Specific Maintenance

Plumbing

- Inspect valves
- Check for leaks
- Flush water heaters
- Clean drains

Electrical

- Test GFCI/AFCI

- Inspect panels
- Check for overheating
- Replace aging fixtures

HVAC

- Replace filters
- Clean coils
- Inspect ducts
- Service annually

Building Envelope

- Inspect sealants
- Check flashing
- Repair cracks
- Maintain waterproofing

Each system has its own needs — ignore them at your peril.

PART II — OPERATIONS

17.6 Understanding Building Operations

Operations include:

- Utilities
- Safety systems
- Access control
- Cleaning
- Waste management
- Landscaping
- Vendor management

Operations determine how smoothly your building functions day-to-day.

17.7 Utility Management

Track:

- Water use
- Electricity
- Gas
- Wastewater
- Solar production (if applicable)

Monitoring utilities helps identify leaks, inefficiencies, and opportunities for savings.

17.8 Safety Systems

Safety systems include:

- Fire alarms
- Sprinklers
- Smoke detectors
- Emergency lighting
- Egress routes
- Security systems

These systems must be inspected regularly and kept in working order.

17.9 Vendor & Service Provider Management

Vendors may include:

- Landscapers
- Cleaners
- Pest control
- Elevator technicians
- HVAC contractors
- Security companies

Use written contracts, clear scopes, and performance reviews.

17.10 Documentation & Recordkeeping

Keep records of:

- Maintenance logs
- Service reports
- Inspections
- Warranties
- Manuals
- Utility bills
- Vendor contracts

Good records reduce costs and support warranty claims.

PART III — LONG-TERM PLANNING

17.11 Why Long-Term Planning Matters

Long-term planning:

- Prevents financial surprises
- Extends system life
- Reduces emergency repairs
- Supports budgeting
- Protects property value

Buildings age — planning keeps you ahead of the curve.

17.12 Capital Improvement Planning

Capital improvements include:

- Roof replacement
- Plumbing riser replacement
- HVAC system upgrades
- Electrical panel upgrades
- Window and door replacement
- Structural repairs

These are major expenses that require long-term budgeting.

17.13 Life-Cycle Planning

Every building component has a life cycle.

Examples:

- Roof: 15–30 years
- Water heater: 8–12 years
- HVAC: 10–20 years
- Plumbing: 40–70 years
- Electrical panels: 25–40 years

Plan replacements before failure — not after.

17.14 Reserve Funds & Financial Planning

For condos, HOAs, and commercial buildings, reserve funds are essential.

A strong reserve plan includes:

- Component inventory
- Remaining useful life
- Replacement cost

- Funding strategy

Underfunded reserves lead to special assessments and financial stress.

17.15 Sustainability & Efficiency Upgrades

Long-term planning should include:

- LED lighting
- High-efficiency HVAC
- Low-flow fixtures
- Solar energy
- Battery storage
- Insulation upgrades
- Smart building systems

Efficiency upgrades reduce operating costs and improve comfort.

PART IV — OWNER TOOLS & CHECKLISTS

17.16 Maintenance Tools

Use:

- Maintenance logs
- Seasonal checklists
- System inventory sheets
- Service contracts
- Inspection forms

Consistency is more important than complexity.

17.17 Operations Tools

Use:

- Utility tracking spreadsheets
- Vendor performance logs
- Safety inspection checklists
- Access control logs

These tools keep operations smooth and predictable.

17.18 Long-Term Planning Tools

Use:

- Life-cycle charts
- Capital improvement plans
- Reserve study templates
- Budget forecasting tools

Planning protects your future.

17.19 A Well-Maintained Building Is a Well-Managed Investment

When you maintain your building proactively, manage operations effectively, and plan for the long term:

- Emergencies decrease
- Costs become predictable
- Systems last longer
- Safety improves
- Property values rise
- Stress disappears

Construction may end — but stewardship continues. With the right structure, tools, and mindset, you can protect your investment for decades to come.

Chapter 18 — Project Management Tools & Templates

Construction management becomes dramatically easier when you use the right tools. Tools create structure. Structure creates clarity. Clarity creates control. Without tools, even the best-planned project becomes chaotic. With tools, even complex projects become manageable, predictable, and far less stressful.

This chapter introduces the essential project management tools and templates every owner should use — and explains how to integrate them into your workflow. These tools are simple, practical, and designed to help you stay organized from start to finish.

PART I — WHY TOOLS MATTER

18.1 Tools Turn Information into Action

Construction generates enormous amounts of information:

- Decisions
- Drawings
- Schedules
- Budgets
- Emails
- Inspections

- Change orders
- Photos

Without a system, this information becomes overwhelming. Tools help you:

- Capture information
- Organize it
- Track it
- Communicate it
- Use it to make better decisions

Tools are not paperwork — they are your roadmap.

18.2 Tools Protect You

Tools protect you from:

- Miscommunication
- Scope creep
- Budget overruns
- Schedule delays
- Disputes
- Poor documentation
- Forgotten decisions

A well-organized owner is a protected owner.

PART II — CORE PROJECT MANAGEMENT TOOLS

18.3 Project Definition Worksheet

This worksheet captures:

- Purpose
- Scope
- Constraints
- Success criteria

It ensures your project starts with clarity.

18.4 Scope Checklist

A detailed checklist that:

- Defines what is included
- Identifies what is excluded

- Clarifies assumptions
- Prevents misunderstandings

A clear scope reduces change orders.

18.5 Budget Worksheet

Your budget worksheet should include:

- Base costs
- Allowances
- Contingencies
- Soft costs
- Indirect costs
- Change order impacts

A budget is a living document — update it regularly.

18.6 Schedule Templates

Essential scheduling tools include:

- Milestone schedule
- Phase schedule
- Decision deadline tracker
- Inspection and permit timeline

These tools help you anticipate decisions and avoid delays.

18.7 Communication Tools

Communication tools include:

- Meeting agendas
- Meeting minutes
- Decision logs
- RFI logs
- Weekly progress reports

These tools keep everyone aligned and accountable.

18.8 Documentation Tools

Documentation tools include:

- Document control logs
- Drawing and revision logs

- Submittal logs
- Daily site reports
- Photo documentation systems

Documentation is your insurance policy.

18.9 Quality Control Tools

Quality tools include:

- Inspection checklists
- Punch list templates
- Material verification logs
- Workmanship standards

Quality is not something you hope for — it's something you verify.

18.10 Change Management Tools

Change management tools include:

- Change order request forms
- Change order logs
- Cost impact worksheets
- Schedule impact worksheets

These tools prevent surprise costs.

18.11 Closeout Tools

Closeout tools include:

- Final punch list
- Warranty log
- As-built documentation checklist
- O&M manual checklist
- Final payment checklist

Closeout is where many projects fall apart — tools keep it organized.

PART III — DIGITAL TOOLS & ONLINE PLATFORMS

18.12 Why Digital Tools Matter

Digital tools:

- Centralize information

- Improve communication
- Reduce errors
- Provide real-time updates
- Make documentation easier
- Support remote collaboration

Digital tools don't replace good management — they enhance it.

18.13 Constructionplace.com Tools

Constructionplace.com provides:

- Checklists
- Worksheets
- Logs
- Budget tools
- Scheduling tools
- Communication templates
- Project dashboards
- Resource libraries

These tools are designed for owners, managers, and professionals — simple enough for beginners, powerful enough for experts.

18.14 Integrating Digital and Paper Tools

Some owners prefer digital tools. Others prefer paper. Most use both.

A hybrid system works best:

- Use digital tools for storage and communication
- Use paper tools for walkthroughs and inspections
- Sync everything regularly

The goal is consistency — not perfection.

PART IV — USING TOOLS EFFECTIVELY

18.15 The Five Rules of Effective Tool Use

1. Use the same tools throughout the project
2. Keep everything in one place
3. Update tools immediately after decisions
4. Share tools with your team
5. Review tools at each phase transition

Tools only work when used consistently.

See "Constructionplace.com" for virtual tools.

18.16 Tools for Owners vs. Tools for Contractors

Owners need tools for:

- Planning
- Budgeting
- Communication
- Documentation
- Quality control

Contractors need tools for:

- Scheduling
- Labor management
- Procurement
- Subcontractor coordination

Your tools complement — not replace — the contractor's tools.

18.17 Tools for Small vs. Large Projects

Small projects need:

- Scope checklist
- Budget worksheet
- Simple schedule
- Punch list

Large projects need:

- Full documentation system
- Detailed schedules
- Multiple logs
- Formal communication tools

Scale your tools to your project — not the other way around.

18.18 Training Your Team to Use Tools

If your team includes:

- Designers

- Contractors
- Consultants
- Property managers
- Committee members

Make sure they understand:

- Which tools you use
- How you use them
- How often they must update them
- Where documents are stored

Tools only work when everyone participates.

PART V — OWNER CHECKLISTS & TEMPLATES

18.19 Essential Checklists

- Project definition checklist
- Scope checklist
- Budget checklist
- Schedule checklist
- Communication checklist
- Quality control checklist
- Closeout checklist

Checklists prevent mistakes.

18.20 Essential Logs

- Decision log
- RFI log
- Change order log
- Budget log
- Inspection log
- Punch list log
- Warranty log

Logs create accountability.

18.21 Tools Turn Chaos into Clarity

When you use the right tools:

- Projects become predictable
- Decisions become easier
- Communication improves
- Costs stay under control
- Quality increases
- Stress decreases

Tools don't just organize your project — they empower you as an owner. They give you confidence, clarity, and control. They turn construction management from something overwhelming into something manageable.

With the right tools, construction management truly becomes easy.

Chapter 19 — Residential Projects

Residential projects are personal. They affect daily life, comfort, safety, and long-term financial stability. Whether you're remodeling a kitchen, replacing plumbing, building an addition, or constructing a new home, residential work requires a unique blend of planning, communication, and emotional management. Unlike commercial or condo projects, residential construction happens where people live — and that changes everything.

This chapter gives homeowners a clear, practical system for planning and managing residential projects of any size, from small repairs to full renovations and new construction.

PART I — UNDERSTANDING RESIDENTIAL PROJECTS

19.1 Why Residential Projects Are Unique

Residential projects involve:

- Personal spaces
- Daily routines
- Family needs
- Emotional decisions
- Budget constraints
- Limited access and staging
- Occupied environments

Homeowners often underestimate the complexity of residential work. The key is structure — not guesswork.

19.2 Types of Residential Projects

Residential projects typically fall into four categories:

1. Repairs
Fixing leaks, electrical issues, HVAC failures, or structural problems.

2. Remodels
Updating kitchens, bathrooms, flooring, or layouts.

3. Additions
Expanding living space, adding bedrooms, or building ADUs.

4. New Construction
Building a home from the ground up.

Each type requires different planning, budgeting, and scheduling strategies.

19.3 The Homeowner's Role

You don't need to be a construction expert. Your role is to:

- Define your goals
- Set a realistic budget
- Choose the right team
- Communicate clearly
- Make timely decisions
- Track progress
- Protect your home and family

Residential projects succeed when homeowners stay engaged — not overwhelmed.

PART II — PLANNING RESIDENTIAL PROJECTS

19.4 Defining Your Project

Start with clarity:

- What problem are you solving?
- What improvements matter most?
- What is your must-have list?
- What is your nice-to-have list?
- What is your budget range?
- What is your timeline?

A clear definition prevents scope creep and emotional overspending.

19.5 Setting a Realistic Budget

Residential budgets must include:

- Base construction costs

- Allowances for finishes
- Contingencies (10–20%)
- Soft costs (design, permits)
- Temporary housing (if needed)
- Indirect costs (storage, moving, cleaning)

Homeowners often underestimate costs — especially finishes. Plan realistically.

19.6 Choosing the Right Delivery Method

For residential projects, the most common delivery methods are:

- Design–Bid–Build (traditional)
- Design–Build (streamlined)
- Owner–Builder (high risk, high involvement)

Choose the method that matches your experience, budget, and comfort level.

19.7 Permits & Approvals

Residential projects often require:

- Building permits
- Electrical permits
- Plumbing permits
- Mechanical permits
- HOA approvals (if applicable)

Never skip permits — they protect you legally and financially.

PART III — WORKING IN OCCUPIED HOMES

19.8 The Realities of Living Through Construction

Expect:

- Dust
- Noise
- Limited access
- Temporary shutdowns
- Disruption to routines
- Safety concerns

Planning reduces stress — but cannot eliminate it entirely.

19.9 Protecting Your Home

Before work begins:

- Remove valuables
- Cover furniture
- Seal off work areas
- Protect flooring
- Establish access routes
- Set rules for pets and children

A protected home is a safer, cleaner, and more efficient jobsite.

19.10 Temporary Living Arrangements

Depending on the project, you may need:

- Temporary kitchens
- Temporary bathrooms
- Off-site housing
- Storage units

Plan ahead to avoid last-minute stress.

PART IV — MANAGING RESIDENTIAL CONTRACTORS

19.11 Choosing the Right Contractor

Look for:

- Residential experience
- Strong communication
- Transparent pricing
- Good references
- Clean, organized job sites

Avoid contractors who:

- Pressure you
- Offer vague bids
- Lack insurance
- Avoid written communication

Your contractor is your partner — choose wisely.

19.12 Reviewing Residential Bids

Residential bids should include:

- Detailed scope
- Material specifications
- Allowances
- Exclusions
- Schedule
- Payment terms
- Warranty information

Never compare bids without aligning scopes first.

19.13 Payment Schedules for Residential Work

A fair payment schedule includes:

- Reasonable deposit (10–20%)
- Progress payments tied to milestones
- Retainage (5–10%)
- Final payment only after punch list completion

Never pay too much upfront.

PART V — QUALITY CONTROL IN HOMES

19.14 Residential Inspection Milestones

Critical inspections include:

- Pre-demo walkthrough
- Rough plumbing
- Rough electrical
- Rough HVAC
- Insulation
- Pre-drywall
- Waterproofing
- Final finishes
- Punch list

Never let walls close without inspections.

19.15 Common Residential Quality Issues

Watch for:

- Uneven flooring
- Poor tile alignment
- Inconsistent paint
- Loose fixtures
- Poor waterproofing
- Incorrect electrical placement
- Plumbing leaks

Small issues become big problems if ignored.

PART VI — SPECIAL RESIDENTIAL PROJECT TYPES

19.16 Kitchens & Bathrooms

These are the most complex residential remodels due to:

- Plumbing
- Electrical
- Ventilation
- Waterproofing
- Cabinetry
- Appliances

They also have the highest return on investment.

19.17 Additions & ADUs

Key considerations:

- Structural integration
- Foundation requirements
- Utility connections
- Zoning restrictions
- Access and staging

Additions require careful planning to blend old and new.

19.18 Aging-in-Place & Accessibility

Consider:

- Wider doorways
- Zero-threshold showers
- Grab bars

- Non-slip flooring
- Lever handles
- Improved lighting

These upgrades improve safety and long-term livability.

PART VII — FINISHING STRONG

19.19 Punch Lists for Residential Projects

Your punch list should include:

- Paint touch-ups
- Cabinet adjustments
- Fixture alignment
- Door and window operation
- Flooring defects
- Appliance testing

Do not rush the final walkthrough.

19.20 Warranties & Maintenance

Residential warranties typically cover:

- Workmanship (1 year)
- Systems (2 years)
- Structural components (10 years)

Track warranty deadlines and maintenance requirements.

19.21 Residential Projects Are Personal — and Manageable

When you use a structured approach:

- Stress decreases
- Costs stay predictable
- Quality improves
- Decisions become easier
- Your home becomes safer, more comfortable, and more valuable

Residential projects don't have to be overwhelming. With the right tools, planning, and communication, homeowners can manage any project with confidence.

If you'd like, I can now:

- Move on to Chapter 21 — Bringing It All Together (Conclusion)

- Create appendices, checklists, and worksheets
- Build a full table of contents for the entire book

Just tell me where you want to go next.

Chapter 20 — Small Commercial Projects

Small commercial projects are the backbone of local economies. They include offices, retail spaces, restaurants, medical suites, warehouses, and service businesses. While smaller in scale than major commercial developments, these projects are often more complex than residential work because they must meet stricter codes, support business operations, and satisfy multiple stakeholders — owners, tenants, customers, inspectors, and sometimes corporate franchisors.

This chapter gives you a clear, practical system for planning and managing small commercial projects with confidence, whether you're renovating a storefront, building out a tenant space, or upgrading a small office.

PART I — UNDERSTANDING SMALL COMMERCIAL PROJECTS

20.1 What Makes Small Commercial Projects Unique

Small commercial projects involve:

- Business operations
- Customer experience
- Accessibility requirements
- Fire and life-safety codes
- Mechanical and electrical demands
- Tight schedules
- Limited downtime
- Lease obligations

These projects must balance speed, cost, compliance, and business continuity.

20.2 Types of Small Commercial Projects

Common project types include:

1. Tenant Improvements (TIs)

Build-outs for new tenants or reconfigurations for existing ones.

2. Renovations & Upgrades

Modernizing finishes, lighting, HVAC, or accessibility.

3. Repairs & Replacements

Fixing plumbing, electrical, roofing, or structural issues.

4. Change of Use Projects

Converting a space from one business type to another (e.g., office → restaurant).

5. Small Additions

Expanding floor area or adding functional spaces.

Each type has different permitting, design, and scheduling needs.

20.3 The Owner's Role in Small Commercial Projects

Owners must:

- Define business goals
- Understand lease obligations
- Coordinate with tenants
- Approve design decisions
- Manage budgets
- Monitor progress
- Ensure compliance

Commercial owners must think like both a landlord and a business operator.

PART II — PLANNING SMALL COMMERCIAL PROJECTS

20.4 Defining the Project

Start with clarity:

- What business need does this project solve?
- What functions must the space support?
- What are the must-have vs. nice-to-have features?
- What is the required timeline?
- What is the budget range?

Commercial projects succeed when business goals drive design — not the other way around.

20.5 Understanding Lease Requirements

Leases often dictate:

- Who pays for improvements
- What work requires landlord approval
- Required contractors
- Insurance requirements

- Restoration obligations
- Allowed hours of construction

Ignoring lease terms can lead to delays, disputes, or unexpected costs.

20.6 Permits & Approvals

Small commercial projects often require:

- Building permits
- Electrical, plumbing, and mechanical permits
- Fire department approvals
- Health department approvals (restaurants, salons, medical)
- ADA compliance reviews
- Landlord approvals

Commercial permitting is stricter than residential — plan accordingly.

20.7 Budgeting for Commercial Work

Budgets must include:

- Construction costs
- Design fees
- Permits and inspections
- Equipment and fixtures
- IT and low-voltage systems
- Signage
- Contingencies (10–20%)
- Temporary relocation or downtime

Commercial budgets must support both the project and the business.

PART III — DESIGNING SMALL COMMERCIAL SPACES

20.8 Functional Design

Design must support:

- Workflow
- Customer experience
- Safety
- Accessibility
- Branding

- Equipment needs

Good design improves efficiency and revenue.

20.9 Code-Driven Design Requirements

Commercial spaces must meet:

- ADA accessibility
- Fire and life-safety codes
- Ventilation and HVAC requirements
- Electrical load requirements
- Plumbing fixture counts
- Egress and occupancy standards

Code compliance drives layout — not preference.

20.10 Specialty Spaces

Some businesses require specialized design:

- Restaurants (grease traps, hoods, refrigeration)
- Medical offices (plumbing, shielding, equipment loads)
- Salons (ventilation, plumbing)
- Retail (lighting, security)
- Offices (IT, acoustics)

Specialty spaces require early coordination with engineers and inspectors.

PART IV — MANAGING SMALL COMMERCIAL CONTRACTORS

20.11 Choosing the Right Contractor

Look for contractors with:

- Commercial experience
- Knowledge of local codes
- Strong communication
- Clean, organized job sites
- Experience with occupied buildings

Avoid residential-only contractors for commercial work.

20.12 Reviewing Commercial Bids

Commercial bids should include:

- Detailed scope
- Material and equipment specifications
- Allowances
- Exclusions
- Schedule
- Insurance requirements
- Safety plan
- Warranty terms

Align scopes before comparing prices.

20.13 Scheduling for Business Continuity

Strategies include:

- Night or weekend work
- Phased construction
- Temporary partitions
- Maintaining customer access
- Minimizing downtime

Commercial schedules must protect revenue.

PART V — QUALITY CONTROL & INSPECTIONS

20.14 Key Inspection Milestones

Critical inspections include:

- Rough plumbing
- Rough electrical
- Rough HVAC
- Fire sprinkler and alarm
- ADA compliance
- Health department (if applicable)
- Final building inspection

Commercial inspectors are thorough — be prepared.

20.15 Common Commercial Quality Issues

Watch for:

- Improper ADA clearances
- Insufficient ventilation
- Undersized electrical systems
- Poor lighting layout
- Inadequate fire stopping
- Incorrect equipment installation

Quality issues can delay occupancy — or shut down operations.

PART VI — SPECIAL CONSIDERATIONS FOR SMALL COMMERCIAL PROJECTS

20.16 Working in Occupied Buildings

Occupied commercial projects require:

- Noise control
- Dust control
- Safe access routes
- Clear signage
- Daily cleanup
- Coordination with tenants and customers

Safety and professionalism matter.

20.17 Equipment & Technology Integration

Commercial spaces often require:

- POS systems
- Security systems
- Wi-Fi and networking
- Audio/visual systems
- Specialty equipment

Coordinate technology early — not at the end.

20.18 Branding & Customer Experience

Small commercial spaces must reflect:

- Brand identity
- Customer flow
- Lighting and ambiance

- Product placement
- Accessibility

Design is part of your marketing strategy.

PART VII — FINISHING STRONG

20.19 Punch Lists for Commercial Projects

Include:

- ADA compliance checks
- Equipment testing
- Lighting and electrical verification
- HVAC balancing
- Fire alarm and sprinkler testing
- Finish quality

Do not rush the final walkthrough.

20.20 Certificates of Occupancy (CO)

Before opening, you must obtain:

- Final inspection approval
- Fire department approval
- Health department approval (if applicable)
- Certificate of Occupancy

No CO = No business operations.

20.21 Small Commercial Projects Drive Big Success

When you use a structured approach:

- Costs stay predictable
- Schedules stay realistic
- Quality improves
- Compliance is assured
- Business downtime is minimized
- Customer experience improves

Small commercial projects may be small in size — but they are big in impact. With the right planning, tools, and communication, you can deliver a space that supports your business, your customers, and your long-term success.

Chapter 21 — Leasehold / Tenant Improvement (TI) Projects

Leasehold or Tenant Improvement (TI) projects are some of the most common — and most misunderstood — types of commercial construction. They involve modifying a leased space to meet the needs of a tenant's business, whether it's an office, retail store, restaurant, medical suite, or service business. These projects must satisfy the tenant, the landlord, the building's systems, the lease agreement, and local codes — all at the same time.

This chapter gives you a clear, practical system for planning and managing TI projects with confidence, whether you are a landlord, tenant, property manager, or business owner.

PART I — UNDERSTANDING TENANT IMPROVEMENT PROJECTS

21.1 What Makes TI Projects Unique

TI projects involve:

- Two (or more) parties with different interests
- Lease obligations
- Strict timelines
- Limited budgets
- Existing building constraints
- Code and accessibility requirements
- Business operations and branding needs

TI projects succeed when expectations are aligned early.

21.2 Types of Tenant Improvements

1. Warm Shell Build-Outs

Space includes basic HVAC, lighting, and walls.

2. Cold Shell Build-Outs

Space is unfinished — no HVAC, no ceilings, minimal utilities.

3. Renovations of Existing Spaces

Updating finishes, reconfiguring layouts, or upgrading systems.

4. Change of Use Projects

Converting a space from one business type to another (e.g., retail → restaurant).

Each type has different cost, schedule, and permitting requirements.

21.3 Who Pays for What?

TI projects often involve:

- Tenant Improvement Allowances (TIAs)
- Landlord contributions
- Tenant contributions
- Shared responsibilities

The lease should clearly define:

- What the landlord pays for
- What the tenant pays for
- What is considered a “building improvement”
- What must be removed at the end of the lease

Never start work without understanding these obligations.

PART II — PLANNING TI PROJECTS

21.4 Understanding the Lease

Before planning begins, review:

- TI allowance amount
- Approval requirements
- Permitted uses
- Construction rules
- Insurance requirements
- Hours of construction
- Restoration obligations
- Signage rules
- Landlord’s contractors (if required)

The lease is the rulebook — ignore it at your own risk.

21.5 Defining the Project

Start with clarity:

- What functions must the space support?
- What equipment is required?
- What are the must-have vs. nice-to-have features?
- What is the required opening date?
- What is the budget?

TI projects succeed when business needs drive design.

21.6 Budgeting for TI (Tenant Improvements) Projects

Budgets must include:

- Construction costs
- Design fees
- Permits and inspections
- IT and low-voltage systems
- Furniture, fixtures, and equipment (FF&E)
- Signage
- Security systems
- Contingencies (10–20%)

TI allowances rarely cover the full cost — plan accordingly.

21.7 Permits & Approvals

TI projects often require:

- Building permits
- Electrical, plumbing, mechanical permits
- Fire department approvals
- Health department approvals (restaurants, salons, medical)
- Landlord approvals

Permitting timelines can make or break your opening date.

PART III — DESIGNING TENANT SPACES

21.8 Functional Design

Design must support:

- Workflow
- Customer experience
- Equipment needs
- Safety
- Accessibility
- Branding

Good design improves efficiency and revenue.

21.9 Code-Driven Design Requirements

TI spaces must meet:

- ADA accessibility
- Fire and life-safety codes
- Ventilation and HVAC requirements
- Electrical load requirements
- Plumbing fixture counts
- Egress and occupancy standards

Code compliance drives layout — not preference.

21.10 Specialty TI Spaces

Some tenants require specialized design:

- Restaurants (grease traps, hoods, refrigeration)
- Medical offices (plumbing, shielding, equipment loads)
- Salons (ventilation, plumbing)
- Retail (lighting, security)
- Offices (IT, acoustics)

Specialty spaces require early coordination with engineers and inspectors.

PART IV — MANAGING TI CONTRACTORS

21.11 Choosing the Right Contractor

Look for contractors with:

- TI experience
- Knowledge of local codes
- Experience working in occupied buildings
- Strong communication
- Clean, organized job sites

Avoid residential-only contractors for TI work.

21.12 Reviewing TI Bids

TI bids should include:

- Detailed scope
- Material and equipment specifications
- Allowances
- Exclusions

- Schedule
- Insurance requirements
- Safety plan
- Warranty terms

Align scopes before comparing prices.

21.13 Scheduling for Business Operations

Strategies include:

- Night or weekend work
- Phased construction
- Temporary partitions
- Maintaining customer access
- Minimizing downtime

TI schedules must protect business continuity.

PART V — QUALITY CONTROL & INSPECTIONS

21.14 Key Inspection Milestones

Critical inspections include:

- Rough plumbing
- Rough electrical
- Rough HVAC
- Fire sprinkler and alarm
- ADA compliance
- Health department (if applicable)
- Final building inspection

TI inspectors are thorough — be prepared.

21.15 Common TI Quality Issues

Watch for:

- Improper ADA clearances
- Undersized electrical systems
- Inadequate ventilation
- Incorrect equipment installation
- Poor lighting layout

- Fire stopping issues

Quality issues can delay occupancy — or shut down operations.

PART VI — SPECIAL CONSIDERATIONS FOR TI PROJECTS

21.16 Working in Occupied Buildings

Occupied TI projects require:

- Noise control
- Dust control
- Safe access routes
- Clear signage
- Daily cleanup
- Coordination with tenants and customers

Professionalism matters.

21.17 Equipment & Technology Integration

TI spaces often require:

- POS systems
- Security systems
- Wi-Fi and networking
- Audio/visual systems
- Specialty equipment

Coordinate technology early — not at the end.

21.18 Branding & Customer Experience

TI spaces must reflect:

- Brand identity
- Customer flow
- Lighting and ambiance
- Product placement
- Accessibility

Design is part of your marketing strategy.

PART VII — FINISHING STRONG

21.19 Punch Lists for TI Projects

Include:

- ADA compliance checks
- Equipment testing
- Lighting and electrical verification
- HVAC balancing
- Fire alarm and sprinkler testing
- Finish quality

Do not rush the final walkthrough.

21.20 Certificates of Occupancy (CO)

Before opening, you must obtain:

- Final inspection approval
- Fire department approval
- Health department approval (if applicable)
- Certificate of Occupancy

No CO = No business operations.

21.21 TI Projects Are High-Impact, High-Value Investments

When you use a structured approach:

- Costs stay predictable
- Schedules stay realistic
- Quality improves
- Compliance is assured
- Business downtime is minimized
- Customer experience improves

TI projects may be limited in size, but they are enormous in impact. With the right planning, tools, and communication, you can deliver a space that supports your business, your customers, and your long-term success.

Chapter 22 — Condo & HOA Projects

Condo and HOA projects are fundamentally different from private residential or commercial projects. They involve shared ownership, shared responsibility, and shared risk — but not always shared understanding. Decisions are made by boards, influenced by committees, and funded by owners who may or may not agree with the direction. This creates a unique environment where governance, transparency, and communication matter just as much as technical expertise.

This chapter gives you a clear, practical system for managing condo and HOA projects with confidence. Whether you are a board member, committee member, property manager, or concerned owner, the principles here will help you protect your building, your investment, and your community.

PART I — UNDERSTANDING CONDO & HOA PROJECTS

22.1 Why Condo Projects Are Different

Condo and HOA projects involve:

- Multiple stakeholders
- Shared financial responsibility
- Legal and fiduciary obligations
- Complex governance structures
- Higher scrutiny
- Public meetings and records
- Long-term maintenance obligations

These factors make condo projects more challenging — and more important to manage correctly.

22.2 The Board's Fiduciary Duty

Board members have a legal obligation to:

- Act in the best interest of all owners
- Use sound judgment
- Avoid conflicts of interest
- Maintain transparency
- Follow governing documents
- Protect the association's assets

Fiduciary duty is not optional — it is the foundation of responsible governance.

22.3 The Role of Owners

Owners have the right to:

- Access information
- Attend meetings
- Review records
- Participate in committees
- Vote on major decisions
- Hold the board accountable

Owners are not passive observers — they are stakeholders with a voice.

22.4 The Role of Property Managers

Property managers:

- Coordinate maintenance
- Manage vendors
- Support the board
- Maintain records
- Communicate with owners

But they do not make decisions. The board does.

PART II — PLANNING & GOVERNANCE

22.5 The Importance of Long-Term Planning

Condo projects require:

- Reserve studies
- Maintenance plans
- Capital improvement plans
- Safety assessments
- Code compliance reviews

Long-term planning prevents emergency assessments and protects property values.

22.6 Transparency and Communication

Transparency builds trust. Boards should:

- Share information openly
- Provide clear meeting agendas
- Document decisions
- Explain project rationale
- Communicate timelines and costs
- Encourage owner participation

Secrecy creates conflict. Transparency creates community.

22.7 Committees: The Owner's Voice

Committees provide:

- Expertise
- Oversight
- Owner representation

- Project support
- Accountability

Committees should be empowered, not ignored.

22.8 Competitive Bidding: Protecting Owners' Money

Competitive bidding:

- Ensures fair pricing
- Prevents favoritism
- Improves quality
- Increases transparency
- Reduces risk

Boards should never award major contracts without competitive bids.

PART III — MANAGING CONDO PROJECTS

22.9 The Unique Challenges of Condo Construction

Condo projects involve:

- Occupied buildings
- Limited access
- Noise restrictions
- Safety concerns
- Coordination with residents
- Staging limitations
- Complex plumbing and mechanical systems

These challenges require careful planning and communication.

22.10 Working in Occupied Buildings

Occupied projects require:

- Clear schedules
- Notice to residents
- Dust and noise control
- Safety barriers
- Temporary access routes
- Daily cleanup

Respect for residents is essential.

22.11 Plumbing and Pipe Replacement in Condos

Plumbing is the most critical system in multi-unit buildings.

Key considerations:

- Aging pipes
- Shared risers
- High risk of leaks
- Insurance implications
- Coordinated replacement during remodels
- Standardized replacement policies

Coordinated pipe replacement saves money and prevents disasters.

22.12 Mechanical and Electrical Systems

Condo systems often include:

- Central HVAC
- Fire alarms
- Sprinklers
- Elevators
- Exhaust systems
- Electrical risers

These systems require specialized expertise and regular inspections.

22.13 Safety and Code Compliance

Safety requirements include:

- Fire protection
- Egress routes
- Structural integrity
- Electrical safety
- Plumbing code compliance
- Accessibility

Boards must prioritize safety — not convenience.

PART IV — FINANCIAL MANAGEMENT

22.14 Reserve Studies: Your Financial Roadmap

A reserve study identifies:

- Major components
- Remaining useful life
- Replacement costs
- Funding requirements

A strong reserve study prevents special assessments and financial crises.

22.15 Special Assessments

Special assessments occur when:

- Reserves are inadequate
- Emergencies arise
- Projects are deferred
- Costs exceed expectations

Special assessments are avoidable with proper planning.

22.16 Insurance Considerations

Condo insurance must cover:

- Common elements
- Building systems
- Liability
- Flood or hurricane risk (if applicable)

Owners must understand what is — and is not — covered.

PART V — OWNER RIGHTS & DISPUTE PREVENTION

22.17 Owner Rights

Owners have the right to:

- Access records
- Review contracts
- Attend meetings
- Participate in decisions
- Challenge improper actions

Owner rights are protected by law.

22.18 Preventing Disputes

Disputes are minimized when boards:

- Communicate clearly

- Document decisions
- Follow governing documents
- Use competitive bidding
- Involve owners early
- Maintain transparency

Most disputes are preventable.

22.19 Handling Conflicts Professionally

When conflicts arise:

- Stay calm
- Focus on facts
- Use documentation
- Refer to governing documents
- Seek mediation if needed

Professionalism protects the community.

22.20 Strong Governance Creates Strong Communities

When condo and HOA projects are managed with transparency, planning, and owner involvement:

- Costs stay predictable
- Safety improves
- Property values rise
- Disputes decrease
- Trust grows
- The community thrives

Condo projects are not just construction projects — they are community projects. With the right structure and leadership, they can be managed smoothly, responsibly, and successfully.

Chapter 23 — Large Commercial Projects

Large commercial projects are complex, high-risk, high-value undertakings that require disciplined planning, strong leadership, and rigorous project management. These projects involve multiple stakeholders, sophisticated building systems, strict regulatory requirements, and significant financial commitments. When managed well, they create long-term value, support business growth, and enhance community infrastructure. When mismanaged, they lead to delays, cost overruns, disputes, and operational disruptions.

This chapter gives you a clear, practical system for planning and managing large commercial projects with confidence — whether you're developing an office building, hotel, retail center, medical facility, educational building, or mixed-use development.

PART I — UNDERSTANDING LARGE COMMERCIAL PROJECTS

23.1 What Makes Large Commercial Projects Unique

Large commercial projects involve:

- Complex building systems
- Multiple design and engineering disciplines
- Large budgets and financing requirements
- Strict regulatory oversight
- Long schedules
- High-risk construction activities
- Extensive coordination
- Public visibility and scrutiny

These projects demand a higher level of structure, documentation, and professional management.

23.2 Types of Large Commercial Projects

Common project types include:

- Office buildings
- Hotels and resorts
- Retail centers and malls
- Medical facilities
- Educational buildings
- Industrial and warehouse facilities
- Mixed-use developments
- Government and institutional buildings

Each type has unique design, code, and operational requirements.

23.3 The Owner's Role in Large Commercial Projects

Owners must:

- Define project goals
- Secure financing
- Select the delivery method

- Hire the project team
- Approve major decisions
- Monitor progress
- Manage risk
- Ensure compliance

Large commercial owners must think strategically — not reactively.

PART II — PLANNING LARGE COMMERCIAL PROJECTS

23.4 Defining the Project Vision

Start with clarity:

- What is the purpose of the project?
- Who will use the building?
- What functions must it support?
- What are the financial goals?
- What is the required timeline?
- What are the success criteria?

A strong vision guides every decision.

23.5 Feasibility Studies

Feasibility studies evaluate:

- Site conditions
- Zoning and land-use restrictions
- Environmental constraints
- Market demand
- Financial viability
- Infrastructure capacity
- Parking requirements

Feasibility determines whether the project should move forward — and how.

23.6 Budgeting for Large Commercial Projects

Budgets must include:

- Construction costs
- Design and engineering fees
- Permits and approvals

- Utility upgrades
- Furniture, fixtures, and equipment (FF&E)
- Technology and security systems
- Contingencies (10–20%)
- Financing costs
- Developer fees
- Insurance and bonding

Large commercial budgets are complex — and must be updated continuously.

23.7 Selecting the Delivery Method

Common delivery methods include:

- Design–Bid–Build
- Design–Build
- Construction Management at Risk (CMAR)
- Integrated Project Delivery (IPD)
- Public–Private Partnerships (P3)

Choose the method that aligns with your risk tolerance, schedule, and team capabilities.

23.8 Permits, Approvals & Regulatory Requirements

Large commercial projects require:

- Building permits
- Environmental approvals
- Fire and life-safety approvals
- Accessibility compliance
- Utility coordination
- Traffic impact studies
- Stormwater management plans
- Health department approvals (if applicable)

Regulatory delays can derail schedules — plan early.

PART III — DESIGNING LARGE COMMERCIAL BUILDINGS

23.9 The Design Team

The design team may include:

- Architects

- Structural engineers
- Mechanical, electrical, and plumbing (MEP) engineers
- Civil engineers
- Landscape architects
- Fire protection engineers
- Acoustical consultants
- Lighting designers
- Technology consultants

Large projects require coordinated, multidisciplinary design.

23.10 Design Phases

Design typically includes:

- Programming
- Schematic design
- Design development
- Construction documents
- Permitting
- Construction administration

Each phase builds on the previous one — and requires owner involvement.

23.11 Code-Driven Design Requirements

Large commercial buildings must meet:

- Fire and life-safety codes
- Structural requirements
- Accessibility standards
- Energy codes
- Mechanical ventilation requirements
- Electrical load requirements
- Egress and occupancy standards

Code compliance drives design decisions.

23.12 Sustainability & Efficiency

Consider:

- LEED certification - LEED certification is a globally recognized rating system that evaluates how sustainably a building is designed, constructed, and operated. Projects earn points for meeting environmental standards in areas such as energy efficiency, water conservation, materials, indoor air quality, and site impact. Higher point totals achieve higher certification levels (Certified, Silver, Gold)
- Energy-efficient HVAC
- Solar and battery systems
- Water conservation
- Smart building systems
- High-performance envelopes

Sustainability reduces operating costs and increases long-term value.

PART IV — MANAGING LARGE COMMERCIAL CONTRACTORS

23.13 Selecting the Right Contractor

Look for contractors with:

- Large commercial experience
- Strong safety records
- Financial stability
- Proven project management systems
- Skilled subcontractor networks
- Transparent communication

Large projects require professional, well-organized contractors.

23.14 Reviewing Commercial Bids

Bids should include:

- Detailed scope
- Material and equipment specifications
- Subcontractor lists
- Schedule
- Safety plan
- Insurance and bonding
- Value engineering options
- Warranty terms

Align scopes before comparing prices.

23.15 Scheduling Large Commercial Projects

Schedules must include:

- Critical path analysis
- Long-lead items
- Phased construction
- Utility coordination
- Inspection timelines
- Weather contingencies

Large commercial schedules are complex — and must be monitored closely.

PART V — QUALITY CONTROL & INSPECTIONS

23.16 Key Inspection Milestones

Critical inspections include:

- Structural inspections
- MEP rough-in inspections
- Fire alarm and sprinkler testing
- Envelope and waterproofing inspections
- Accessibility compliance
- Energy code inspections
- Final building inspection

Quality issues can delay occupancy — or create long-term liability.

23.17 Common Large Commercial Quality Issues

Watch for:

- Waterproofing failures
- HVAC balancing issues
- Electrical load problems
- Fire stopping deficiencies
- Poor coordination between trades
- Inconsistent finishes
- Incomplete commissioning

Quality control must be continuous — not reactive.

PART VI — SPECIAL CONSIDERATIONS FOR LARGE COMMERCIAL PROJECTS

23.18 Safety & Risk Management

Large projects require:

- Safety plans
- Daily safety meetings
- OSHA compliance
- Site security
- Risk assessments
- Insurance and bonding

Safety is non-negotiable.

23.19 Technology & Systems Integration

Large buildings require:

- Security systems
- Access control
- Networking and Wi-Fi
- Audio/visual systems
- Building automation systems
- Energy management systems

Technology must be coordinated early — not added at the end.

23.20 Commissioning & Testing

Commissioning verifies:

- HVAC performance
- Electrical systems
- Plumbing systems
- Fire and life-safety systems
- Building automation
- Energy efficiency

Commissioning ensures the building performs as designed.

PART VII — FINISHING STRONG

23.21 Punch Lists for Large Commercial Projects

Punch lists must include:

- System testing
- ADA compliance
- Fire and life-safety verification
- Finish quality
- Equipment testing
- Mechanical balancing
- Electrical load testing

Do not rush the final walkthrough.

23.22 Certificates of Occupancy (CO)

Before opening, you must obtain:

- Final inspection approval
- Fire department approval
- Health department approval (if applicable)
- Certificate of Occupancy

No CO = No operations.

23.23 Large Commercial Projects Require Leadership, Structure & Discipline

When you use a structured approach:

- Costs stay predictable
- Schedules stay realistic
- Quality improves
- Compliance is assured
- Risk is reduced
- Long-term performance increases

Large commercial projects are complex — but manageable. With the right planning, tools, and communication, you can deliver a building that supports your business, your tenants, and your long-term success.

Chapter 24 — High-Rise Condo Projects

High-rise condominium projects are among the most complex, politically sensitive, and technically demanding construction projects an owner or board will ever manage. These buildings contain hundreds of residents, interconnected systems, aging infrastructure, and strict safety requirements. Decisions affect not just one home — but an entire vertical community.

This chapter gives you a clear, practical system for planning and managing high-rise condo projects with confidence. Whether you're a board member, committee member, property manager, or concerned owner, the principles here will help you protect your building, your investment, and your community.

PART I — UNDERSTANDING HIGH-RISE CONDO PROJECTS

24.1 What Makes High-Rise Projects Unique

High-rise projects involve:

- Shared systems (plumbing, electrical, HVAC, fire protection)
- Vertical infrastructure (risers, shafts, chases)
- Limited access and staging
- Occupied environments
- Strict safety and fire-life-safety codes
- Complex permitting
- Multiple stakeholders
- High financial impact

These projects require more planning, more communication, and more discipline than any other project type.

24.2 The Board's Legal & Fiduciary Responsibilities

Boards must:

- Act in the best interest of all owners
- Maintain the building's safety and integrity
- Follow governing documents
- Ensure competitive bidding
- Maintain transparency
- Avoid conflicts of interest
- Document decisions

High-rise boards carry significant legal responsibility — and must act accordingly.

24.3 The Role of Owners

Owners have the right to:

- Access information
- Attend meetings

- Review records
- Participate in committees
- Vote on major decisions
- Hold the board accountable

High-rise projects succeed when owners are informed and engaged.

PART II — PLANNING HIGH-RISE PROJECTS

24.4 Long-Term Planning Is Essential

High-rise buildings require:

- Reserve studies
- Capital improvement plans
- Safety assessments
- Plumbing and riser evaluations
- Electrical capacity studies
- Elevator modernization plans

Deferred maintenance in a high-rise becomes exponentially more expensive.

24.5 Understanding Building Systems

High-rise systems include:

- Plumbing risers
- Electrical risers
- Fire sprinklers
- HVAC systems
- Exhaust and ventilation
- Elevators
- Structural components
- Building envelope

These systems are interconnected — a failure in one can affect the entire building.

24.6 The Importance of Pre-Project Investigations

Before starting any major project, investigate:

- Existing conditions
- As-built drawings (often inaccurate)
- Pipe materials and age

- Electrical capacity
- Fire-life-safety requirements
- Structural limitations
- Access and staging constraints

Investigations prevent surprises — and surprises are expensive.

PART III — PLUMBING & RISER PROJECTS

24.7 Why Plumbing Is the #1 Risk in High-Rises

Plumbing failures in high-rises cause:

- Flooding
- Mold
- Insurance claims
- Unit displacement
- Lawsuits
- Special assessments

A single leak can affect multiple floors.

24.8 Coordinated Riser Replacement

The most cost-effective strategy is:

- Replace risers during unit remodels
- Standardize materials and methods
- Require owners to upgrade when walls are open
- Maintain a building-wide replacement plan

This approach saves millions over time.

24.9 Emergency Plumbing Repairs

High-rise emergency repairs require:

- Immediate shut-off
- Access to multiple units
- Skilled plumbers
- Clear communication
- Documentation

Emergency repairs are disruptive — but manageable with structure.

PART IV — MANAGING HIGH-RISE CONTRACTORS

24.10 Choosing the Right Contractor

Look for contractors with:

- High-rise experience
- Strong safety records
- Knowledge of vertical systems
- Experience working in occupied buildings
- Clear communication
- Clean, organized job sites

High-rise work is not for inexperienced contractors.

24.11 Reviewing High-Rise Bids

Bids should include:

- Detailed scope
- Access and staging plans
- Safety plans
- Unit entry protocols
- Material specifications
- Schedule
- Insurance and bonding
- Warranty terms

Align scopes before comparing prices.

24.12 Scheduling in Occupied High-Rises

Schedules must account for:

- Noise restrictions
- Elevator access
- Stacking of units
- Vertical phasing
- Resident notifications
- Inspection timelines

High-rise schedules are complex — and must be managed tightly.

PART V — QUALITY CONTROL & SAFETY

24.13 Key Inspection Milestones

Critical inspections include:

- Plumbing rough-in
- Electrical rough-in
- Fire sprinkler and alarm
- Waterproofing
- Envelope and window systems
- Final inspections

High-rise inspectors are thorough — be prepared.

24.14 Fire-Life-Safety Requirements

High-rise buildings must meet:

- Fire alarm standards
- Sprinkler requirements
- Smoke control systems
- Egress and stairwell standards
- Emergency lighting
- Fire stopping

Fire-life-safety is non-negotiable.

24.15 Common High-Rise Quality Issues

Watch for:

- Improper fire stopping
- Poor waterproofing
- Incorrect pipe slopes
- Electrical overloads
- HVAC balancing issues
- Inconsistent finishes
- Noise transmission problems

Quality issues can affect dozens of units.

PART VI — COMMUNICATION & GOVERNANCE

24.16 Transparency Builds Trust

Boards should:

- Share information openly
- Provide clear meeting agendas
- Document decisions
- Explain project rationale
- Communicate timelines and costs
- Encourage owner participation

Secrecy creates conflict. Transparency creates community.

24.17 Working with Property Managers

Property managers must:

- Coordinate access
- Manage vendors
- Communicate with residents
- Maintain records
- Support the board

But they do not make decisions — the board does.

24.18 Owner Communication During Projects

Owners need:

- Advance notice
- Clear schedules
- Access instructions
- Safety information
- Contact points
- Regular updates

Good communication reduces complaints and increases cooperation.

PART VII — FINISHING STRONG

24.19 Punch Lists in High-Rise Projects

Punch lists must include:

- System testing
- Fire-life-safety verification
- Finish quality

- Equipment testing
- Plumbing and electrical checks

Do not rush the final walkthrough.

24.20 Documentation & Closeout

Closeout should include:

- As-built drawings (sometimes Record Drawings)
- Warranty documents
- O&M manuals
- Fire-life-safety certifications
- Inspection reports
- Final budget
- Maintenance recommendations

Closeout is critical for long-term building performance.

24.21 High-Rise Projects Require Leadership, Structure & Community

When you use a structured approach:

- Costs stay predictable
- Schedules stay realistic
- Quality improves
- Safety is assured
- Disputes decrease
- Owner trust increases
- The building performs better for decades

High-rise condo projects are complex — but manageable. With the right planning, communication, and governance, you can protect your building, your investment, and your community.

APPENDICES

These appendices contain the core tools that make construction management simple, structured, and predictable. Each tool aligns with a chapter in the book and can be used for real projects, classroom assignments, or professional training.

Appendix A — Tools, Worksheets & Checklists

This appendix contains the core tools that support the construction management system presented in this book. Each worksheet and checklist is designed to help owners, boards, managers, and students apply the principles of clear definition, structured planning, disciplined communication, and proactive quality control. These tools may be photocopied, adapted, or reproduced for personal, educational, or project use.

NOTES

A01. Project Reediness Checklist

The Project Readiness Checklist helps owners confirm that all essential information, decisions, and preparations are in place before moving forward with design, bidding, or construction. It walks you through key readiness factors — including scope clarity, budget alignment, schedule expectations, site conditions, required approvals, and available documentation — to ensure nothing critical has been overlooked.

A1. Project Readiness Checklist

(Pre-Design and Pre-Bid Requirements)

Project Information

Project Name: ___________________________________

APN Number: ___________________________

Project Location / Address: ___________________________

Prepared By: ______________________

Date: ___________________________

1. Project Definition

☐ Purpose of the project clearly defined

☐ Scope of work drafted (in-scope and out-of-scope identified)

☐ Project goals documented and measurable

☐ Constraints identified (budget, schedule, regulatory, site)

☐ Success criteria established

Notes: _______________________________________

2. Site and Existing Conditions

☐ Site inspected and documented

☐ Existing drawings, surveys, or as-builts collected

☐ Utility locations identified

☐ Hazardous materials assessed (if applicable)

☐ Access, staging, and logistics constraints identified

☐ Photos of existing conditions taken and archived

Notes: ______________________________________

3. Regulatory Requirements

☐ Zoning requirements reviewed

☐ Building code requirements identified

☐ Permit requirements confirmed

☐ Environmental or special inspections identified

☐ HOA/Board approvals required (if applicable)

☐ Required professional stamps identified (architect/engineer)

Notes: ____

4. Budget and Funding

☐ Preliminary budget established

☐ Funding source confirmed

☐ Allowances and contingencies identified

☐ Cost escalation considerations reviewed

☐ Long-lead items identified

Notes: ____

5. Design Requirements

☐ Design professional selected (or selection process underway)

☐ Program requirements documented

☐ Performance requirements defined (quality, durability, systems)

☐ Material preferences or standards identified

☐ Sustainability or energy requirements identified

☐ Required drawings and specifications listed

Notes: ____

6. Procurement and Contracting

☐ Contract type selected (Lump Sum, T&M, NTE, etc.)

☐ Bidder qualification requirements defined

☐ Insurance and bonding requirements established

☐ RFP/RFQ documents drafted

☐ Bid alternates and allowances identified

☐ Evaluation criteria established

Notes: ____

7. Schedule Requirements

☐ Target start date established

☐ Target completion date established

☐ Milestones identified

☐ Permit timelines accounted for

☐ Long-lead procurement integrated

Notes: ____

8. Risk Identification

☐ Site risks documented

☐ Financial risks identified

☐ Schedule risks identified

☐ Regulatory risks identified

☐ Mitigation strategies drafted

Notes: ____

9. Communication and Governance

☐ Project directory created

☐ Roles and responsibilities defined

☐ Decision-making authority established

☐ Reporting requirements defined

☐ Meeting schedule established

Notes: ____

10. Pre-Bid Package Completeness

☐ Drawings complete to required level

☐ Specifications complete

☐ Scope of work finalized

☐ Bid form prepared

☐ Addenda process defined

☐ Pre-bid meeting scheduled (if applicable)

Notes: ____

11. Final Readiness Confirmation

☐ All documents reviewed for accuracy and completeness

☐ All stakeholders notified and aligned

☐ All required approvals obtained

☐ Project is ready for design or bidding

Approvals

Owner / Owner's Representative

Name: ______________________________

Signature: ___________________________

Date: _________________

Project Manager / Construction Manager

Name: ______________________________

Signature: ___________________________

Date: _________________

Design Professional (if applicable)

Name: ______________________________

Signature: ___________________________

Date: _________________

A02. Project Definition Worksheet

A simple, structured form that helps owners clearly define a project's purpose, scope, goals, constraints, and success criteria before design, bidding, or construction begins. It ensures everyone starts with the same understanding and reduces costly misunderstandings later.

A2. Project Definition Worksheet

(Purpose, Scope, Goals, Constraints, and Success Criteria)

Project Information

Project Name: ____

APN Number: ____________________________

Project Location / Address: ________________________________

Prepared By: ____________________________

Date: ____________________________

1. Purpose

Describe why this project is being undertaken and the problem or opportunity it addresses.

2. Scope

Define what is included in the project and what is not included.

In-Scope Work

Out-of-Scope Work

3. Goals

List the primary goals the project must achieve. These should be specific, measurable, and aligned with the project's purpose.

☐ ____

☐ ____

☐ ____

☐ ____

☐ ____

4. Constraints

Identify the limitations that will affect planning, design, cost, schedule, or execution.

Budget Constraints

Schedule Constraints

Regulatory / Permitting Constraints

Site / Operational Constraints

Other Constraints

5. Success Criteria

Define how success will be measured at completion. These criteria guide decision-making throughout the project.

☐ Completed within approved budget

☐ Completed within approved schedule

☐ Meets quality and performance requirements

☐ Meets safety and regulatory requirements

☐ Achieves intended functional use

☐ Satisfies owner/user expectations

☐ Other: ____

Additional Notes: ____

6. Approvals

Owner / Owner's Representative

Name: ______________________________

Signature: ______________________________

Date: ________________

Project Manager / Construction Manager

Name: ______________________________

Signature: ______________________________

Date: ________________

Design Professional (if applicable)

Name: ______________________________

Signature: ______________________________

Date: ________________

A03. Project Definition Worksheet

A structured planning tool that helps owners and boards clearly outline the essential elements of a project before design, bidding, or construction begins. It guides you through defining the project's purpose, scope, budget expectations, schedule needs, site conditions, risks, and success criteria so everyone starts with the same understanding.

A3. Project Definition Worksheet

Project Name:

Project Location:

Prepared By:

Date:

1. Purpose of the Project

- What problem are we solving?
- What opportunity are we creating?
- What is the desired outcome?

2. Project Goals

- Functional goals:
- Aesthetic goals:
- Operational goals:
- Financial goals:

3. Scope Summary

- Spaces affected:
- Systems affected (plumbing, electrical, HVAC, etc.):
- Special requirements:

4. Constraints

- Budget constraints:
- Schedule constraints:
- Access or occupancy constraints:
- Regulatory constraints:

5. Success Criteria

- How will we know the project is successful?

A04. Scope Checklist

The Scope Checklist is a structured tool that helps owners clearly identify what work is included — and not included — in their project before design, bidding, or construction begins. It walks you through each major project component so nothing important is overlooked, assumed, or left vague.

A4. Scope Checklist

Use this checklist to ensure all elements of the project are clearly defined before design or bidding.

General

- □ Project purpose defined
- □ Affected spaces identified
- □ Existing conditions reviewed
- □ Required permits identified

Architectural

- □ Layout changes
- □ Walls, ceilings, floors
- □ Doors, windows
- □ Finishes and materials

Mechanical / Electrical / Plumbing (MEP)

- □ HVAC modifications
- □ Electrical load requirements
- □ Lighting plan
- □ Plumbing fixtures and piping
- □ Fire sprinkler adjustments

Specialty Items

- □ Equipment requirements
- □ Technology and low-voltage systems
- □ Security systems
- □ Accessibility requirements

Owner-Provided Items

- □ Furniture
- □ Fixtures
- □ Appliances
- □ Specialty equipment

A05. Budget Worksheet

Helps you outline costs, allowances, and contingencies so you start with a clear financial plan.

Constructionplace.com offers a comprehensive General Requirements Calculator and the Magic Budget Calculator App

A5. Budget Worksheet

Construction Costs

- Demolition: $________
- Structural: $________
- Architectural: $________
- Mechanical: $________
- Electrical: $________
- Plumbing: $________
- Fire protection: $________
- Finishes: $________
- Equipment: $________
- Contingency (10–20%): $________

Soft Costs

- Design fees: $________
- Engineering fees: $________
- Permits and approvals: $________
- Testing and inspections: $________
- Project management: $________

Other Costs

- Temporary relocation: $________
- Storage: $________
- IT and low-voltage: $________
- Signage: $________

Total Estimated Budget: $________________

A06. Schedule Template

The Schedule Template helps owners outline the major tasks, milestones, and deadlines that make up their project timeline. It provides a simple, organized structure for mapping out what needs to happen, when it should happen, and how long each phase is expected to take.

A6. Schedule Template

Milestones

- Project definition complete: __________
- Design complete: __________
- Permits submitted: __________
- Permits approved: __________
- Construction start: __________
- Rough-in inspections: __________
- Final inspections: __________
- Substantial completion: __________
- Final completion: __________

Notes

- Long-lead items:
- Access restrictions:
- Phasing requirements:

NOTES

A07. Communication Log

Use this log to track conversations, commitments, and next steps

Date	Person	Topic	Decision/Action	Follow-Up Date	Action

A08. Decision Log

Documenting decisions prevents confusing and disputes

Decision	Date	Made By	Reason	Impact (Cost/Schedule)	Notes

A09. RFI Log (Request for Information)

RFIs clarify design intent and prevent mistakes

RFI No.	Date Submitted	Submitted By	Question	Response	Date Answered

A10. Change Order Log

Track all changes to maintain budget and schedule control

Change Order No.	Description	Cost	Schedule Impact	Date Submitted	Date Approved	Notes

A11. Inspection Checklist

The Inspection Checklist provides owners with a structured, step-by-step tool for verifying that work is completed correctly, safely, and in accordance with the plans, specifications, and industry standards. It guides users through key inspection points at each phase of the project — from pre-construction conditions to in-progress work to final closeout — ensuring that critical items are reviewed before they are concealed or finalized.

A11. Inspection Checklist

Rough-In Inspections

- ☐ Plumbing rough-in
- ☐ Electrical rough-in
- ☐ HVAC ductwork
- ☐ Fire sprinkler rough-in
- ☐ Framing inspection

Pre-Cover Inspections

- ☐ Waterproofing
- ☐ Fire stopping
- ☐ Insulation
- ☐ Penetrations sealed

Final Inspections

- ☐ Electrical final
- ☐ Plumbing final
- ☐ Mechanical final
- ☐ Fire alarm and sprinkler
- ☐ Accessibility compliance
- ☐ Final building inspection

A12. Punch List Template

The Punch List Template provides a clear, organized format for documenting incomplete, incorrect, or outstanding items that must be addressed before final project acceptance. It helps owners, contractors, and inspectors record each issue, assign responsibility, track status, and set deadlines for correction.

Item No.	Location	Description	Assigned To	Date Identified	Date Completed	Notes

A13. Warrantee Log

The Warranty Log provides owners with a centralized record of all warranties associated with the project, including coverage details, start and end dates, responsible parties, and required maintenance actions. It organizes warranty information by system, equipment, or component, making it easy to track obligations and quickly locate documentation when issues arise.

Use the Guarantee and Warrantee feature on Constructionplace.com

Item.	Contractor	Warranty Period	Expiration Date	Notes

Appendix B — Sample Forms & Templates

These templates help owners, boards, and instructors standardize communication and documentation.

B01. RFQ Scoring Sheet

RFQ = Request for Qualifications - It is a formal procurement document used when an owner wants to select the most qualified contractor, consultant, or professional based on qualifications — not price.

B1. RFQ Scoring Sheet

Project Information

Project Name:

____

APN Number: ______________________________

Project Location / Address: ______________________________

RFQ Number (if applicable): ______________________________

Evaluator Name: ______________________________

Date: ______________________________

1. Evaluation Criteria and Weights

Assign weights to each criterion. Total must equal 100%. (Example weights shown)

Evaluation Criteria	Weigh %
Technical Approach	30
Experience	25
Key Personnel	20
Past Performance	10
Submission Quality	5
Capacity	10
Other (specify):	
Total Weight	**100%**

2. Scoring Matrix

Score each proposer on a consistent scale (e.g., 1–10). Multiply Proposer Score × weight to determine weighted score. (Proposer Score x Weight =

Example

If a proposer 1 scores 8 on Technical Approach (weighted at 30%):[8 times 0.30 = 2.4]

That 2.4 becomes part of their total weighted score.

Proposer	Technical Approach	Experience	Key Personnel	Past Performance	Quality	Capacity
1 Proposer Score 8	2.4					
2 Proposer Score (1-10)						
2 Proposer Score (1-10)						

3. Qualitative Evaluation Notes

Use this section to record strengths, weaknesses, and discussion points.

Proposer 1

Strengths: ______________________________

Weaknesses: ______________________________

Notes: ______________________________

Proposer 2

Strengths: ______________________________

Weaknesses: ______________________________

Notes: ______________________________

Proposer 3

Strengths: ______________________________

Weaknesses: ______________________________

Notes: ______________________________

4. Ranking and Recommendation

Rank	Proposer	Total Score from Scoring Matrix above	**Recommended (Yes/No)**	
			Yes	No

Rationale for Recommendation:

5. Approvals

Evaluator

Name: ____________________________________

Signature: ____________________________________

Date: ____________________

Owner / Owner's Representative

Name: ____________________________________

Signature: ____________________________________

Date: ____________________

.

NOTES

B02. Request for Proposal (RFP) Template

The Request for Proposal (RFP) Template provides owners with a clear, organized format for requesting detailed proposals from qualified contractors, designers, or consultants. It outlines the project scope, requirements, expectations, and submission instructions so bidders understand exactly what information to provide.

Use Constructionplace.com virtual RFPs

B2. Request for Proposal (RFP) Template

Use on Constructionplace.com

Project Information

Date: ______________________________

APN Number: ______________________________

Project Title: ____

Project Location / Address: ________________________________

Issued By (Owner/Agency): ________________________________

Issued To (Contractor/Vendor): ______________________________

Invitation to Propose

You are invited to submit a Cost Proposal for the project described below. Complete all sections and return your proposal by the deadline indicated.

Proposal Documents & Delivery

Latest Revision Date: ____________________

Addenda Issued (Numbers): ______________

Proposal Due Date: _____________________

Proposal Due Time: _____________________

Plans and Specifications Available From

Name: ______________________________

Phone: ______________________________

Email: ______________________________

Submit Proposal To

Name: ______________________________

Phone: ______________________________

Email: ______________________________

Description of Work

Type of Proposal Requested

☐ Lump Sum ☐ Time and Materials ☐ Not to Exceed

Other: ____

Unit Percentage Fees (if applicable)

☐ Additions (labor and materials) ☐ Deductions (labor and materials)

Requested Alternates and Allowances

Schedule Requirements

Start Date: ______________________ Start Time: ________________

Completion Date: ____________________ Completion Time: __________

Delivery Date (if applicable): ________________________________

Other Requirements: ____

Include:

☐ Lead time for long-lead items

☐ Number of calendar days required to complete the work

Bonding & Insurance

☐ Bid Bond ☐ Performance Bond ☐ Payment Bond

Actual Cost of Bonds (not included in base bid): ________________________

Additional Insured Parties (quantity): ________________________________

☐ See continuation page for insurance limits

Other Requirements

Pre-Proposal Site Inspection: ☐ Yes ☐ No

Inspection Date: ____________________ Time: _________________

Special Instructions:

Attachments

☐ 2.2 Procedural Memorandum

☐ 2.3 Proposal / Agreement

☐ 2.3a Terms and Conditions

☐ 2.4 Continuation Page

☐ Other:

A clear, concise format for soliciting contractor bids. Use on Constructionplace.com

B03. Bid Comparison Matrix

The Bid Comparison Matrix helps owners evaluate contractor proposals side-by-side using a clear, structured format. It breaks each bid into comparable categories — pricing, exclusions, schedule, qualifications, assumptions, and value-added items — so differences are easy to spot and hidden costs don't slip through.

Use Constructionplace.com Compare Bids

B3. Bid Comparison Matrix

A side-by-side comparison tool for evaluating contractor proposals.

Project Information

Date: ________________________________

APN Number: __________________________

To: __________________________________

From: ________________________________

Project Location / Address (Job Number):

Bid Opening or Tabulating Cost Proposals

The following table is used to record and compare bids received for the project. Enter each bidder in the order bids are opened or no opening order.

Use Comparing Bids on Constructionplace.com

Form Option (Opening Order) 1

Bid Opening Order	Bidder's Name	Description	Base Bid	Completion Time	Alternate (Adds)	Alternate (Deducts)

Form Option 2

	Bidder's Name	Bidder's Name	Bidder's Name
Base Bid			
Alternates			
Allowances			
Exclusions			
Schedule			
Subcontractors			
Warrantee			
Bonding Rate			
Bonding Capacity			
Other			

Negotiating With Professionals

Use this table to evaluate proposals from architects, engineers, consultants, or other professionals. Record pricing, timelines, and discussion notes to support selection.

Professional's Name	Price	Completion Time	Comments Discussion	Date Identified	Order of Preference	Notes

NOTES

B04. Contractor Evaluation Form

The Contractor Evaluation Form provides a structured way for owners to assess a contractor's qualifications, experience, reliability, and overall fit for the project. It guides you through key evaluation factors — including licensing, insurance, past performance, references, financial stability, staffing, safety record, and proposed approach — so nothing important is overlooked.

B4. Contractor Evaluation Form

Criteria-based scoring for selecting the right contractor.

Hiring Construction Professionals

Project Information

Date: ______________________

APN Number: ________________

To: ____

From: ____

Project Location / Address: ____

Prime or Main Contractor — Self-Assessment Checklist

Use this checklist to determine whether you should hire a prime contractor or construction manager. Mark one box for each question.

Question	Yes	No	Maybe
Do you understand the scope of work necessary to begin and complete your project?	☐	☐	☐
Are you capable of preparing a written scope of work or specifications for your project?	☐	☐	☐
Do you have the ability to qualify trade professionals and/or subcontractors?	☐	☐	☐
Do you have the time to schedule, coordinate, and inspect your project?	☐	☐	☐
Is your project free of structural alterations or improvements?	☐	☐	☐
Will your specialty contractors supply all materials, labor, and clean-up without your assistance?	☐	☐	☐
Are you able and willing to prepare, submit, and obtain all required building permit documents?	☐	☐	☐
Are you willing to assume full	☐	☐	☐

Question	Yes	No	Maybe
responsibility for your project?			
Are you capable of reviewing and approving progress and final payments to contractors?	☐	☐	☐
Do you understand the importance of securing certificates of insurance and lien releases?	☐	☐	☐
Totals			

NOTES

B05. Meeting Agenda & Minutes Template

The Meeting Agenda & Minutes Template provides a clear, organized format for planning project meetings and documenting what was discussed, decided, and assigned. It helps owners and project teams outline topics in advance, stay focused during the meeting, and record key decisions, action items, responsibilities, and deadlines.

B5. Meeting Agenda & Minutes Template

A structured format for productive project meetings.

Meeting Information

Meeting Date: ______________________________

APN Number: ______________________________

Start Time: ______________________________

End Time: ______________________________

Project Location / Address: ______________________________

Meeting Type

☐ Pre-Construction Meeting ☐ Course of Construction Meeting

☐ Project Closeout Meeting ☐ One-Year Inspection

Topics for Discussion

☐ ______________________________

☐ ______________________________

☐ ______________________________

☐ ______________________________

☐ ______________________________

Other: ______________________________

Emergency Contact Information

Classification	Name/Company	Telephone	Email

Project Closeout Checklist

☐ Final inspection completed

☐ Punch list issued

☐ Punch list completed

☐ All permits closed

☐ Warranties received

☐ O&M manuals received

☐ As-built drawings received

☐ Final lien releases received

☐ Final payment approved

☐ Other: ____

NOTES

B06. Progress Payment Request Form

The Progress Payment Request Form provides a clear, standardized way for contractors to request payment for work completed to date. It helps owners verify that billed work aligns with actual progress, approved schedules of values, and any required supporting documentation such as invoices, receipts, or lien releases.

B6. Progress Payment Request Form

Project Name:

Contractor:

Invoice Number:

Billing Period:

Date Submitted:

1. Contract Summary

- Original contract amount: $________
- Approved change orders: $________
- Revised contract amount: $________

2. Work Completed

- Work completed this period: $________
- Work completed to date: $________
- Retainage withheld: $________

3. Supporting Documentation

- ☐ Schedule update
- ☐ Photos
- ☐ Change order log
- ☐ Inspection reports

4. Certification

I certify that the work billed has been completed as described.

Contractor Signature: ________________________

Date: ________________________

B07. Progress Payment Request Verification and Approval Form

The Progress Payment Request Verification & Approval Form provides owners with a structured, transparent process for reviewing and approving contractor payment requests. It guides users through key verification steps — confirming completed work, checking supporting documentation, validating change orders, reviewing lien releases, and ensuring contract compliance — before any payment is authorized.

Revised Contract Amount (USD): ____________________

Previous Payments (USD): ____________________

Current Payment Requested (USD): ____________________

Balance Remaining (USD): ____________________

Approval

Verified By: ____________________ Date: __________

Title / Role: ____________________

Approved By: ____________________ Date: __________

Title / Role: ____________________

Comments: ____________________

NOTES

B7. Progress Payment Request Verification and Approval Form

A simple form for verifying and approving payment requests.

Project Information

Project Name: ______________________________

APN Number: ______________

Project Location / Address: ______________________________

Contractor / Vendor: ______________________________

Invoice / Payment Request No.: ______________________

Invoice Date: ______________

Amount Requested (USD): ______________________

Description of Work or Services

Provide a brief description of the work, materials, or services covered by this payment request.

Verification Checklist

Mark each item after reviewing supporting documentation.

☐ Work completed matches the approved scope of work

☐ Quantities and unit prices match the contract or approved change orders

☐ All required inspections for this phase have been completed

☐ Supporting documents provided (invoices, receipts, timesheets, etc.)

☐ Change orders (if any) have been approved prior to billing

☐ Retention withheld in accordance with contract

☐ Lien releases received for prior payments

☐ Insurance and license remain current

☐ No unresolved deficiencies or punch-list items related to this billing

☐ Payment request amount is mathematically accurate

Notes: ______________________________

Financial Summary

Contract Amount (USD): ______________________

Approved Change Orders (USD): ______________________

B08. Substantial Completion Certificate

The Substantial Completion Certificate documents the point at which a project is sufficiently complete for the owner to occupy or use the work for its intended purpose. It records the official date of substantial completion, identifies any remaining punch-list items. The certificate helps establish warranty start dates, shift insurance and maintenance obligations, and provide a clear reference for final payment procedures.

It ensures all parties agree on the project's status and creates an essential checkpoint in the closeout process.

B8. Substantial Completion Certificate

Documents when the project is ready for occupancy.

Project Information

Project Name: ______________________________

APN Number: ______________________

Project Location / Address: _________________________

Contractor: ________________________________

Owner / Agency: ______________________________

Contract Number (if applicable): ______________________

Certification of Substantial Completion

The undersigned hereby certifies that the project identified above has reached Substantial Completion as of:

Date of Substantial Completion: ______________________

Substantial Completion is defined as the stage in the progress of the work when the project is sufficiently complete, in accordance with the contract documents, so the owner can occupy or utilize the work for its intended use.

Scope of Work Covered

Describe the portion(s) of the project deemed substantially complete.

Punch-List Items

The following items remain to be completed, corrected, or delivered:

Item No.	Description of Work or Corrected	Responsible Party	Comments Discussion	Target Completion Date

Additional Notes:

Warranties, Manuals, and Closeout Documents

☐ Warranties received

☐ Operations & Maintenance manuals received

☐ As-built drawings received

☐ Final inspections completed

☐ Required testing completed

☐ Other: ____

Owner's Acknowledgment

The owner acknowledges receipt of this certificate and accepts the project as substantially complete as of the date stated above. Responsibility for security, utilities, insurance, and maintenance transfers to the owner unless otherwise noted.

Exceptions or Conditions:

Signatures

Contractor

Name: ______________________________

Signature: ______________________________

Date: ________________

Owner / Owner's Representative

Name: ______________________________

Signature: ______________________________

Date: ________________

Design Professional (if applicable)

Name: ______________________________

Signature: ______________________________

Date: ________________

☐ Required testing completed

☐ Other: ____

Owner's Acknowledgment

The owner acknowledges receipt of this certificate and accepts the project as substantially complete as of the date stated above. Responsibility for security, utilities, insurance, and maintenance transfers to the owner unless otherwise noted.

Exceptions or Conditions:

Signatures

Contractor

Name: ______________________________

Signature: ______________________________

Date: ________________

Owner / Owner's Representative

Name: ______________________________

Signature: ______________________________

Date: ________________

Design Professional (if applicable)

Name: ______________________________

Signature: ______________________________

Date: ________________

B09. Final Completion Certificate

The Final Completion Certificate documents that all contract work — including punch-list items, corrective actions, inspections, testing, and closeout requirements — has been fully completed in accordance with the contract documents. It records the official date of final completion and confirms that all deliverables, warranties, O&M manuals, as-builts, and financial obligations have been satisfied.

B9. Final Completion Certificate

Confirms all work is complete and warranties begin.

Project Information

APN Number: ______________________________

Project Name: ____

Project Location / Address: ________________________________

Contractor: ____

Owner / Agency: ____

Contract Number (if applicable): _____________________________

Certification of Final Completion

The undersigned certifies that the project identified above has achieved Final Completion as of:

Date of Final Completion: ______________________________

Final Completion is defined as the point at which all contract work, punch-list items, inspections, testing, documentation, and closeout requirements have been fully completed in accordance with the contract documents.

Confirmation of Completed Work

All work required under the contract has been completed, including:

☐ All punch-list items resolved

☐ All corrective work completed

☐ All inspections passed

☐ All testing completed and approved

☐ All warranties submitted

☐ All O&M manuals submitted

☐ All as-built drawings submitted

☐ All permits closed

☐ All lien releases received

☐ Final payment application submitted

☐ Other: ____

Notes:

Final Financial Summary

Original Contract Amount (USD): ________________________________

Approved Change Orders (USD): ________________________________

Revised Contract Amount (USD): ________________________________

Total Payments to Date (USD): ________________________________

Retention Released (USD): ________________________________

Final Payment Due (USD): ________________________________

Owner's Acceptance

The owner acknowledges that all work has been completed in accordance with the contract documents and accepts the project as fully complete.

Exceptions or Conditions (if any):

Signatures

Contractor

Name: ________________________________

Signature: ________________________________

Date: ____________________

Owner / Owner's Representative

Name: ________________________________

Signature: ________________________________

Date: ____________________

Design Professional (if applicable)

Name: ________________________________

Signature: ________________________________

Date: ____________________

Notes:

Final Financial Summary

Original Contract Amount (USD): ___________________________

Approved Change Orders (USD): ___________________________

Revised Contract Amount (USD): ___________________________

Total Payments to Date (USD): ___________________________

Retention Released (USD): ___________________________

Final Payment Due (USD): ___________________________

Owner's Acceptance

The owner acknowledges that all work has been completed in accordance with the contract documents and accepts the project as fully complete.

Exceptions or Conditions (if any):

Signatures

Contractor

Name: ___________________________

Signature: ___________________________

Date: ________________

Owner / Owner's Representative

Name: ___________________________

Signature: ___________________________

Date: ________________

Design Professional (if applicable)

Name: ___________________________

Signature: ___________________________

Date: ________________

B10. Warranty Start/End Certificate

The Warranty Start/End Certificate documents the official beginning and expiration dates of all warranties associated with the project. It provides a clear record of coverage for materials, equipment, systems, and workmanship, along with any manufacturer-specific warranty terms or conditions.

B10. Warranty Start/End Certificate

Project Information

Project Name: ______________________________

APN Number: ______________________________

Project Location / Address: ______________________________

Contractor: ______________________________

Owner / Agency: ______________________________

Contract Number (if applicable): ______________________________

Certification of Warranty Period

The undersigned certifies that the warranties associated with the project identified above begin and end on the dates listed below.

Warranty Start Date: ______________________________

Warranty End Date: ______________________________

Warranties begin upon substantial or final completion unless otherwise stated in the contract documents.

Warranty Coverage Summary

List each warranty provided, including equipment, materials, workmanship, systems, and manufacturer warranties.

Item/System	Description of Warrantee	Provider Manufacturer	Start Date	End Date

Additional Notes:

Documents Provided

☐ Warranty certificates

☐ Manufacturer warranty documents

☐ Operations & Maintenance manuals

☐ As-built drawings

☐ Service and maintenance requirements

☐ Other: ____

Owner Responsibilities

The owner acknowledges receipt of all warranty documents and understands the following obligations:

- Maintain the project in accordance with manufacturer and contractor requirements
- Notify the contractor promptly of any warranty-related issues
- Retain all warranty documentation for the duration of the warranty period
- Follow required maintenance schedules to avoid voiding warranties

Exceptions or Conditions: ______________________________________

Signatures

Contractor

Name: ___________________________________

Signature: ___________________________________

Date: ____________________

Owner / Owner's Representative

Name: ___________________________________

Signature: ___________________________________

Date: ____________________

Design Professional (if applicable)

Name: ___________________________________

Signature: ___________________________________

Date: ____________________

B11. Warranty Claim Form

The Warranty Claim Form provides owners with a clear, organized way to report defects, performance issues, or failures covered under project warranties. It guides users to document the problem, identify the affected system or component, describe when and how the issue was discovered, and attach supporting evidence such as photos, reports, or maintenance records.

B11. Warranty Claim Form

Project Information

Project Name: ____________________

APN Number: ____________________

Project Location / Address: ____________________

Owner / Agency: ____________________

Contractor: ____________________

Contract Number (if applicable): ____________________

Claim Information

Date of Claim Submission: ____________________

Warranty Start Date: ____________________

Warranty End Date: ____________________

Item / System Affected: ____________________

Location of Issue: ____________________

Description of Problem or Defect

Provide a clear description of the issue, including when it was first observed and any conditions present at the time.

Supporting Documentation

Check all that apply and attach copies.

☐ Photos

☐ Videos

☐ Manufacturer warranty documents

☐ Service or maintenance records

☐ Inspection reports

☐ Other: ____________________

Impact on Use or Safety

Describe how the issue affects the use, performance, or safety of the project or system.

Requested Action

☐ Repair

☐ Replacement

☐ Inspection / Evaluation

☐ Other: ____

Preferred Response Date: ______________________________

Contractor / Manufacturer Response (to be completed by recipient)
Date Received: ______________________________

Reviewed By: ______________________________

Findings:

Action to Be Taken:

☐ Covered under warranty

☐ Not covered under warranty

☐ Additional information required

☐ Other: ____

Target Completion Date: ______________________________

Signatures

Owner / Owner's Representative

Name: ______________________________

Signature: ______________________________

Date: ________________

Contractor / Manufacturer Representative

Name: ______________________________

Signature: ______________________________

Date: ________________

Appendix C — Courses and Education

This appendix offers a simple, flexible syllabus for using Construction Management Made Easy in courses, workshops, certificate programs, and professional development.

C01. Sample Course Syllabus (8-Week Format)

C1. Sample Course Syllabus (8-Week Format)

Course Title

Construction Management Fundamentals: A Practical Owner-Focused Approach

Course Description

This course introduces students to the core principles of construction management using Construction Management Made Easy as the primary text. Students learn how to define, plan, budget, schedule, manage, and successfully complete construction projects of any size. Emphasis is placed on owner empowerment, practical tools, communication, documentation, and real-world application.

Course Learning Objectives

By the end of this course, students will be able to:

- Define project goals, scope, budget, and schedule
- Understand delivery methods and team roles
- Use essential project management tools and checklists
- Evaluate bids and select contractors
- Manage communication and documentation
- Oversee construction progress and quality
- Manage changes, delays, and disputes
- Complete closeout and warranty processes
- Apply principles to residential, commercial, TI, and high-rise projects

Required Text

Construction Management Made Easy (Second Edition), by W Gary Westernoff

Weekly Course Outline (8-Week Format)

Week 1 — Introduction to Construction Management

- Owner's role
- Project phases
- Tools and mindset
- Chapters 1–4

Activity: Define a mock project

Discussion: Why do projects fail

Week 2 — Project Definition & Planning

- Scope, budget, schedule
- Delivery methods
- Permits and approvals
- Chapters 5–8

Assignment: Scope checklist

Week 3 — Team Selection & Pre-Construction

- Designers, contractors, consultants
- Bidding and evaluation
- Pre-construction meetings
- Chapters 9–11

Activity: Contractor evaluation matrix

Week 4 — Quality Control & Inspections

- Workmanship standards
- Inspection milestones
- Documentation
- Chapters 12–14

Assignment: Inspection checklist

Week 5 — Managing Construction

- Communication
- Progress tracking
- Safety
- Changes, delays, disputes
- Chapters 15–17

Activity: Change order analysis

Week 6 — Closeout & Warranties

- Punch lists
- Final payment
- Warranties
- Chapters 17–18

Assignment: Punch list creation

Week 7 — Project Types

- Residential
- Small commercial
- Tenant improvements
- Large commercial
- High-rise condo projects
- Chapters 20–24

Activity: Case study comparison

Week 8 — Bringing It All Together

- Tools and templates
- Final project presentations
- Chapter 25

Final Project: Manage a mock project from start to finish

NOTES

C02. Learning Objectives (Detailed)

Students will learn to:

- Apply structured project management tools
- Communicate effectively with designers and contractors
- Interpret drawings, specifications, and proposals

- Track decisions, changes, and progress
- Conduct inspections and verify quality
- Navigate closeout and warranty processes
- Understand differences between project types
- Manage risk, safety, and compliance

C03. Suggested Assignments & Activities

Instructors may choose any combination of the following:

Assignments

- Project Definition Worksheet
- Scope Checklist
- Budget Worksheet
- Schedule Template
- Contractor Evaluation Form
- Change Order Analysis
- Punch List Creation
- Final Project (Mock Project Management)

Activities

- Site visit
- Guest speaker
- Case study review
- Constructionplace.com tool demonstration
- Group discussion on project failures

C04. Course Assessment Options

Suggested Grading Breakdown

- Participation: 20%
- Weekly assignments: 40%
- Final project or exam: 40%

Optional Quizzes

- Terminology (from Appendix E Glossary of Construction Terms)
- Project phases
- Delivery methods
- Quality control

- Closeout

C05. Instructor Notes

- This course is suitable for students with or without construction experience.
- Emphasize practical application over theory.
- Encourage students to use the book's tools on real or hypothetical projects.
- Reinforce the owner-empowerment philosophy throughout.
- Direct instructors to the full Instructor's Guide on Constructionplace.com for expanded materials.

Appendix D — Resources & Further Reading

A curated list of resources to support deeper learning and practical application.

D01. Constructionplace.com Tools & Templates

A comprehensive collection of practical tools designed to help owners, managers, and representatives plan, manage, and monitor construction projects. Includes worksheets, checklists, dashboards, forms, and project management aids that align directly with the processes described in this book. These tools support real-world decision-making and help users avoid costly mistakes.

D02. Construction Management Made Easy by W. Gary Westernoff (ISBN 0-9668245-0-4)

A foundational guide that simplifies the construction process for owners and managers. This book introduces essential concepts, responsibilities, and best practices in clear, accessible language. It serves as a companion to the tools and frameworks presented throughout this new edition.

D03. Construction Like Sushi by W. Gary and Taemi Westernoff (ISBN 978-0-9668245-1-3)

A creative, analogy-driven exploration of construction concepts, using the art of sushi-making to explain complex project management ideas. This book offers a fresh, engaging perspective that helps readers understand sequencing, preparation, teamwork, and quality control in a memorable way.

D04. Constructionplace.com Blog and FAQs

An evolving library of articles, insights, and answers to common construction questions. The blog provides timely guidance on project planning, budgeting, contractor selection, risk management, and owner responsibilities. The FAQs offer quick, practical explanations for issues that frequently arise during construction projects.

External Industry References

These authoritative resources provide additional depth and context for readers who want to explore professional standards, best practices, and industry frameworks.

D05. CMAA — Construction Management Standards of Practice

Published by the Construction Management Association of America, this document outlines the core principles, responsibilities, and best practices of professional construction management. It is widely used by owners, agencies, and CM practitioners to establish consistent expectations and performance standards.

D06. PMI — Construction Extension to the PMBOK® Guide

A specialized supplement to the Project Management Institute's PMBOK® Guide, tailored specifically to the construction industry. It expands on project management processes, risk management, procurement, and stakeholder coordination in the context of complex construction projects.

D07. AIA Contract Documents (A-Series & B-Series)

The American Institute of Architects publishes industry-standard contract forms that define roles, responsibilities, and relationships between owners, architects, and contractors. These documents are widely recognized and serve as a foundation for fair, transparent, and well-structured project agreements.

D08. OSHA Construction Standards (29 CFR 1926)

The Occupational Safety and Health Administration's regulatory framework for construction safety. These standards outline essential requirements for jobsite protection, hazard mitigation, equipment use, and worker safety. They are critical for ensuring compliance and reducing risk on any construction project.

D09. Lean Construction Institute — Last Planner® System Resources

A collection of tools, guides, and research materials focused on improving workflow reliability, collaboration, and productivity in construction. The Last Planner® System is widely adopted for its ability to reduce waste, improve scheduling accuracy, and enhance team coordination.

Appendix E — Glossary of Construction Terms

This updated glossary expands on the First Edition and reflects the broader scope of the Second Edition, including residential, commercial, tenant improvement, and high-rise condo projects. It is designed for owners, boards, managers, students, and professionals who want to understand construction without technical jargon.

Activity (1) A scheduling term (2) The smallest work unit within a project; the basic building block of a project. (see Project)

ADA The Americans with Disabilities Act which gives civil rights protection to individuals with disabilities similar to those provided to individuals on the basis of race, color, sex, national origin, age, and religion. It guarantees equal opportunity for individuals with disabilities in public accommodations, employment, transportation, State and local government services, and telecommunications.

Addendum (Addenda) Written information adding to, clarifying or modifying the bidding documents. An addendum is generally issued by the owner to the contractor during the bidding process and as such, addenda are intended to become part of the contract documents when the construction contract is executed.

Agent One authorized by a client (principal) to act in his/her stead or behalf and owes the client a "fiduciary duty" (Trust). Example: Construction Manager for fee but classified as an independent contractor for tax purposes. A construction manager for fee does not have any financial responsibility whereas a construction manager at-risk does have financial risk similar to a general contractor.

Agreement An arrangement between the parties regarding a method of action.

Allowance A budget placeholder for items not yet fully specified at the time of contracting. The final cost is adjusted up or down once actual selections or quantities are known.

Alterations (1) A term used to describe partial construction work performed within an existing structure (2) Remodeling without a building addition.

Alternate Bid Amount stated in the bid to be added or deducted from the base bid amount proposed for alternate materials and/or methods of construction.

Application for Payment Contractor's written request for payment for completed portions of the work and, for materials delivered or stored and properly labeled for the respective project.

Architect One who designs and supervises the construction of buildings or other structures.

Architects Basic Services A recognized series of phases performed by an architect as follows: 1st Schematic Design Phase, 2nd Design Development Phase, 3rd Construction Document Phase, 4th Bidding or Negotiated Phase, 5th Construction Phase.

Architect-Engineer An individual or firm offering professional services as both architect and engineer.

Architectural Drawing A line drawing showing plan and/or elevation views of the proposed building for the purpose of showing the overall appearance of the building.

As-Built Drawings (also known as Record Drawings) Contract drawings marked up to reflect changes made during the construction process. It is good practice to make ***As-Built drawings*** by marking the changes on reproducible drawings such sepias for duplication purposes later.

As-Built Verification A field review confirming that installed work matches the contractor's as-built drawings and the approved design. Used to validate accuracy before closeout.

Backflow Preventer A device that stops contaminated water from flowing backward into the potable water system. Required for health and safety compliance.

Base Building Systems The core mechanical, electrical, plumbing, structural, and life-safety systems provided by the building owner or developer before tenant improvements.

Bid (1) An offer or proposal of a price (2) The amount offered or proposed.

Bid Bond A written form of security executed by the bidder as principal and by a surety for the purpose of guaranteeing that the bidder will sign the contract, if awarded the contract, for the stated bid amount.

Bid Date/Time The due date and time set by the owner, architect or engineer for receiving bids.

Bid Form A standard written form furnished to all bidders for the purpose of obtaining the requested information and required signatures from the authorized bidding representatives.

Bid Opening The actual process of opening and tabulating bids submitted within the prescribed bid date/time and conforming to the bid procedures. A Bid Opening can be open (where the bidders are permitted to attend) or closed (where the bidders are not permitted to attend). (See Bid Date/Time)

Bid Price The stipulated sum stated in the bidder's bid.

Bidding Documents The published advertisement or written invitation to bid, instructions to bidders, the bid form and the proposed contract documents including any acknowledged addenda issued prior to receipt of bids.

Bidding Period The calendar period allowed from issuance of bidding requirements and contract documents to the prescribed bid date/time. (See Bid Date/Time)

Bidding Requirements The written minimum acceptable requirements set forth by the owner to the contractor during bidding process. The owner usually reserves the right to reject a bid if the Bidding Requirements are not met. (See Bidding Documents)

Bid Shopper A buyer or client who seeks to play one proposed supplier or subcontractor against the other for the purpose of reducing a purchase price.

Bid Tabulation A summary sheet listing all bid prices. (See Bid Form)

Bid Time (see Bid Date/Time)

Bond (see Bid Bond; Contract Bond; Contract Payment Bond; Contract Performance Bond; Labor and Material Payment Bond; Performance Bond; Subcontractor Bond; surety)

Bonding Company A properly licensed firm or corporation willing to execute a surety bond, or bonds, payable to the owner, securing the performance on a contract either in whole or in part; or securing payment for labor and materials.

Booster Pump A pump that increases water pressure in buildings where municipal supply is insufficient to reach upper floors or distant fixtures.

Branch Line A smaller pipe that extends from a main riser or trunk line to serve individual fixtures or equipment.

Budget (Construction Budget) (1) An itemized summary of estimated or intended expenditures for a given period of time (2) The total sum of money allocated for a specific project.

Budget Reconciliation A periodic comparison of projected costs versus actual expenditures to confirm alignment with the approved budget and identify variances early.

Building (1) To form by combining materials or parts (2) A structure enclosed within a roof and within exterior walls housing, shelter, enclosure and support of individuals, animals, or real property of any kind.

Building Code The legal requirements set up by the prevailing various governing agencies covering the minimum acceptable requirements for all types of construction. (See Codes)

Building Envelope (Sometimes referred to as Building Shell) (1) The waterproof elements of a building, which enclose conditioned spaces through which thermal energy may be transferred to or from the exterior. (2) The outer structure of the building. (See Tenant and Leasehold improvements for building interiors)

Building Inspector/Official A qualified government representative authorized to inspect construction for compliance with applicable building codes, regulations and ordinances. Courts have ruled that building inspections are exempt from errors and omissions liabilities.

Building Permit A written document issued by the appropriate governmental authority permitting construction to begin on a specific project in accordance with drawings and specifications approved by the governmental authority.

Building Process A term used to express every step of a construction project from its conception to final acceptance and occupancy.

Capital Improvement A major upgrade or replacement that extends the life, value, or performance of a building system. Typically funded through reserves or special assessments.

Change Order A written document between the owner and the contractor signed by the owner and the contractor authorizing a change in the work or an adjustment in the contract sum or the contract time. A change order may be signed by the architect or engineer, provided they have written authority from the owner for such procedure and that a copy of such written authority is furnished to the contractor upon request. The contract sum and the contract time may be changed only by change order. A change order may be in the form of additional compensation or time; or less compensation or time known as a Deduction (from the contract) the amount deducted from the contract sum by change order.

Change Order Proposal (See Change order) A change order proposal is the written document before it has been approved and effected by the Contractor and Owner. A change order proposal can be issued by either the contractor or the owner. The change order proposal becomes a change order only after it has been approved and effected by the Contractor and Owner.

Change Order Request A written document issued by the owner requesting an adjustment to the contract sum or an extension of the contract time; generally issued by the architect or owners' representative.

Closeout Package The complete set of documents delivered at project completion, including warranties, manuals, as-builts, test reports, and maintenance requirements.

Codes Prevailing regulations, ordinances or statutory requirements set forth by governmental agencies associated with building construction practices and owner occupancy, adopted and administered for the protection of public health, life safety and welfare. (See Building Code)

Cold Shell A tenant space delivered without HVAC, lighting, interior walls, or finished systems. Requires full build-out by the tenant.

Commissioning (Cx) is a structured quality-assurance process for new construction that verifies building systems are designed, installed, tested, and operating according to design intent and performance requirements. It includes design review, installation checks, functional performance testing, correction of deficiencies, and delivery of complete operating documentation. Cx is enforced through contract requirements, building codes, third-party commissioning oversight, and owner controls tied to payment, substantial completion, and warranty obligations. Contractors must complete all testing, correct failures, and provide documentation before the project can be accepted or occupied. (See **Retro-Commissioning (RCx)** for existing Building systems)

Common Elements Areas or systems owned collectively by all unit owners, such as roofs, elevators, lobbies, and structural components.

Competitive Bidding A transparent procurement process where multiple qualified contractors submit proposals, enabling owners to compare scope, cost, and value.

Conflict of Interest A situation where a board member, manager, or contractor has competing personal or financial interests that could compromise impartial decision-making.

Contingency A reserved portion of the budget set aside for unforeseen conditions, design gaps, or owner-requested changes.

Construction Documents All drawings, specifications and addenda associated with a specific construction project.

Construct To assemble and combine construction materials and methods to make a structure.

Construction The act or process of constructing.

Construction Cost (1) The direct contractor costs for labor, material, equipment, and services; contractors overhead and profit; and other direct construction costs.

Construction cost does not include the compensation paid to the architect and engineer and consultants, the cost of the land, rights-of-way or other costs which are defined in the contract documents as being the responsibility of the owner. (See Soft Costs)

Construction Documents A term used to represent all drawings, specifications, addenda, and other pertinent construction information associated with the construction of a specific project.

Construction Documents Phase The third phase of the architect's basic services wherein the architect prepares working drawings, specifications and bidding information. Depending on the architect's scope of services the architect may assists the owner in the preparation of bidding forms, the conditions of the contract and the form of agreement between the owner and contractor.

Construction Document Review The owners review of the borrowers construction documents (plans and specifications), list of materials, and cost breakdowns for the purpose of confirming that these documents and estimates are feasible and are in accordance with the proposed loan or project appraisal.

Construction Inspector (see Project Representative)

Construction Management Organizing and directing men, materials, and equipment to accomplish the purpose of the designer.

Construction Management Contract A written agreement wherein responsibilities for coordination and accomplishment of overall project planning, design and construction are given to a construction management firm. The building team generally consists of the owner, contractor and designer or architect.

Construction Phase The fifth and final phase of the architect's basics services, which includes the architect's general administration of the construction contract(s).

Consultant One hired by the owner or client to give professional advice.

Cost Breakdown (see Schedule of Values)

Cost Codes A numbering system given to specific kinds of work for the purpose of organizing the cost control process of a specific project.

Cost of Work All costs incurred by the contractor in the proper performance of the work required by the plans and specifications for a specific project.

Cost Plus Contract (see Cost Plus Fee Agreement)

Cost Plus Fee Agreement (Cost-Plus) A written agreement with the owner under which the contractor or the architect and engineer is reimbursed for his/her direct and indirect costs and, in addition, is paid a fee for his services. The fee is usually stated as a stipulated sum or as a percentage of cost.

Contract (1) An agreement between two or more parties, especially one that is written and enforceable by law (2) The writing or document containing such an agreement.

Contract Administration The contractual duties and responsibilities of the architect and engineer during the construction phase of a specific project.

Contract Bond A written form of security from a surety company, on behalf of an acceptable prime or main contractor or subcontractor, guaranteeing complete execution of the contract and all supplemental agreements pertaining thereto and for the payment of all legal debts pertaining to the construction of the project.

Contract Date (see date of agreement)

Contract Documents A term used to represent all executed agreements between the owner and contractor; any general, supplementary or other contract conditions; the drawings and specifications; all addenda issued prior to execution of the contract; and any other items specifically stipulated as being included in the contract documents.

Contract Over-run (under-run) The difference between the original contract price and the final completed cost including all adjustments by approved change order.

Contract Payment Bond A written form of security from a surety company to the owner, on behalf of an acceptable prime or main contractor or subcontractor, guaranteeing payment to all persons providing labor, materials, equipment, or services in accordance with the contract.

Contract Performance Bond A written form of security from a surety company to the owner, on behalf of an acceptable prime or main contractor or subcontractor, guaranteeing the completion of the work in accordance with the terms of the contract.

Contract Period The elapsed number of working days or calendar days from the specified date of commencing work to the specified date of completion, as specified in the contract.

Contract Sum The total agreeable amount payable by the owner to the contractor for the performance of the work under the contract documents. (see Change Order)

Contract Time The time period set forth established in the contract documents for completing a specific project; usually stated in working days or calendar days. The contract time can only be adjusted by valid time extensions through change order.

Contractual Liability The liability assumed by a party under a contract.

Contractor A properly licensed individual of company that agrees to furnish labor, materials, equipment and associated services to perform the work as specified for a specified price.

Contractor's Option A written provision in the contract documents giving the contractor the option of selecting certain specified materials, methods or systems without changing in the contract sum.

Contractor's Qualification Statement A written statement of the Contractor's experience and qualifications submitted to the Owner during the contractor selection process. The American Institute of Architects publishes a standard Contractor's Qualification Statement form for this purpose.

Contracting Officer An official representative of the owner with specific authority to act in his behalf in connection with a specific project.

Critical Path The set of activities that must be completed on time for the project completion date to be met. Activities on the critical path have no slack time.

Critical Path Delay A delay that affects the project's longest sequence of dependent tasks, directly extending the overall completion date.

Critical Path Method (C.P.M.) A planning scheduling and control line and symbol diagram drawn to show the respective tasks and activities involved in constructing a specific project.

CSI Construction Specification Institute

CSI Master Format The CSI Master Format is a system of numbers and titles for organizing construction information into a regular, standard order or sequence. By establishing a master list of titles and numbers Master Format promotes standardization and thereby facilitates the retrieval of information and improves construction communication. It provides a uniform system for organizing information in project manuals, for organizing project cost data, and for filing product information and other technical data.

Currant Date Line A vertical line on the chart indicating the currant date.

Daily Construction Report A written document and record that has two main purposes: (1) they furnish information to off-site persons who need and have a right to know important details of events as they occur daily and hourly, and (2) they furnish historical documentation that might later have a legal bearing in cases of disputes. Daily reports should be as factual and impersonal as possible, free from the expression of personal opinions and feelings. Each report should be numbered to correspond with the working days established on the progress schedule. In the event of no-work days, a daily report should still be made, stating "no work today" (due to rain, strike, or other causes). The report includes a description of the weather; a record of the total number of employees, subcontractors by name, work started and completed today, equipment on the job site, job progress today, names and titles of visitors, accidents and/or safety meetings, and a remarks column for other job-related information.

Date of Agreement (1) Usually on the front page of the agreement (2) If not on front page it may be the date opposite the signatures when the agreement was actually signed (3) or when it was recorded (4) or the date the agreement was actually awarded to the contractor.

Date of Commencement of the Work The date established in a written notice to proceed from the owner to the contractor.

Date of Substantial Completion The date certified by the architect when the work or a designated portion thereof is sufficiently complete, in accordance with the contract documents, so the owner may occupy the work or designated portion thereof for the use for which it is intended.

Demising Coordination The alignment of walls, utilities, and systems at the boundary between tenant spaces to ensure proper separation, fire rating, and service distribution.

Demising Walls The boundaries that separate your space from your neighbors' and from the public corridor.

Design A graphical representation consisting of plan views, interior and exterior elevations, sections, and other drawings and details to depict the goal or purpose for a building or other structure.

Design-Build Construction When a Prime or Main contractor bids or negotiates to provide Design and Construction services for the entire construction project.

Design-Construct Contract A written agreement between and contractor and owner wherein the contractor agrees to provide both design and construction services.

Design-Development Phase The second phase of the architect's basic services wherein the architect prepares drawings and other presentation documents to fix and describe the size and character of the entire project as to architectural, structural, mechanical and electrical systems, materials and other essentials as may be appropriate; and prepares a statement of probable construction cost.

Detail (1) An individual part or item (2) A graphical scale representation (drawing at a larger scale) of construction part(s) or item(s) showing materials, composition and dimensions.

Direct Cost (or expense) All items of expense directly incurred by or attributable to a specific project, assignment or task. Direct Costs, Hard Costs, and Construction Costs are synonymous. (See Construction Costs and Hard Costs)

Drawings (1) A term used to represent that portion of the contract documents that graphically illustrates the design, location and dimensions of the components and elements contained in a specific project (2) A line drawing.

Dry Stack A vertical pipe that carries air or exhaust but does not contain water under normal operation.

Due Diligence The investigative process owners undertake before approving a project—reviewing scope, costs, risks, contracts, and contractor qualifications.

Duration The length of an activity, excluding holidays and other non-working days.

Energy Efficiency The use of systems, materials, and practices that reduce energy consumption while maintaining performance and comfort.

Engineer (see Professional Engineer)

Envelope Testing Diagnostic testing of the building's exterior (windows, walls, roofs) to confirm air- and water-tightness and identify leaks or failures.

Estimate (1) To calculate approximately the amount, extent or value of something (2) To form an opinion of estimated costs.

Estimate of Construction Cost, Detailed A calculation of costs prepared on the basis of a detailed analysis of materials and labor for all items of work, as contrasted with an estimate based on current area, volume or similar unit costs. *195

Estimating A process of calculating the amount of material, labor and equipment required for a given project necessary to complete the work as specified.

Expansion Tank A tank that absorbs pressure fluctuations in a closed water system, preventing damage to pipes and equipment.

Fast Track Construction (Fast Tracking) A method of construction management, which involves a continuous design-construction operation. When a prime or main contractor starts the construction work BEFORE the plans and specifications are complete. (See Design-Build Construction)

Fiduciary Duty The legal obligation of board members and managers to act in the best interests of the ownership, with loyalty, care, and transparency.

Field Order A written order effecting a minor change or clarification in the work not involving an adjustment to the contract sum or an extension of the contract time.

Field Report (see Daily Construction Report)

Field Work Order A written request to a subcontractor or vendor, usually from the general or main contractor, site for services or materials.

Final Acceptance The action of the owner accepting the work from the contractor when the owner deems the work completed in accordance with the contract requirements. Final acceptance is confirmed by the owner when making the final payment to the contractor.

Final Inspection A final site review of the project by the contractor, owner or owner's authorized representative prior to issuing the final certificate for payment.

Final Payment The last payment from the owner to the contractor of the entire unpaid balance of the contract sum as adjusted by any approved change orders. (see Final Acceptance)

Finish Date The date that an activity or project is completed.

Fire Pump A dedicated pump that boosts water pressure for fire sprinkler and standpipe systems to meet life-safety requirements.

Fire Riser A vertical pipe that distributes water to fire sprinkler systems on each floor.

Fit-Out The process of completing interior spaces—including partitions, finishes, lighting, and systems—to make them ready for occupancy.

Fixed Fee A set contract amount for all labor, materials, equipment and services; and contractors overhead and profit for all work being performed for a specific scope of work.

Fixed Limit of Construction Costs A construction cost ceiling agreed to between the owner and architect or engineer for designing a specific project. (See Budget)

Float The amount of time a task can be delayed without affecting the project's critical path or completion date.

FF&E (1) An abbreviation for furniture, fixtures and equipment (2) Items classified as personal property rather than real property (3) An abbreviation generally associated with interior design and planning of retail stores or office facilities.

Force Majeure Events beyond the contractor's control—such as natural disasters or government actions—that may justify schedule extensions.

Gantt Chart The schedule of activities for a project. A Gantt Chart shows start and finish dates, critical and non-critical activities, slack time, and predecessor relationships.

General Conditions A written portion of the contract documents set forth by the owner stipulating the contractor's minimum acceptable performance requirements including the rights, responsibilities and relationships of the parties involved in the performance of the contract. General conditions are usually included in the book of specifications but are sometimes found in the architectural drawings.

General Contractor Properly licensed individual or company having primary (prime) responsibility for the work.

General Contracting (the traditional method) When a prime or main contractor bids the entire work AFTER the final design, plans and specifications are complete and have been approved by the owner. (See Design-Build Construction and Fast Track Construction)

Green Building A building designed and constructed to reduce environmental impact through energy efficiency, water conservation, and sustainable materials.

Hard Costs (see Construction Costs and Direct Costs)

Independent Contractor One free from the influence, guidance, or control of another or others and does not owe a "fiduciary duty". Example: architect, engineer, prime or main contractor, construction manager at-risk.

Improvements (1) A term sometimes used to describe TI'S or Tenant Improvements. (2) Improvements can be in the form of new construction or remodel work. (see TI'S)

Indemnification (1) The act of indemnifying. (2) The condition of being indemnified.

Indirect Cost (or expense) A contractor's or consultant's overhead expense; expenses indirectly incurred and not chargeable to a specific project or task. The terms Indirect costs and soft costs are synonymous. (See Soft Costs)

Indoor Air Quality (IAQ) The condition of air inside a building, influenced by ventilation, filtration, humidity, and pollutant levels.

Inspection (1) The act of inspecting. (2) An official examination or review of the work completed or in progress to determine its compliance with contract requirements.

Inspection List (punch list) A list prepared by the owner or his/her authorized representative of items of work requiring immediate corrective or completion action by the contractor.

Inspection Report Sometimes used to describe an *Inspection List*. (see Inspection List)

Inspector One who is appointed or employed to inspect something.

Interior Finish A term used to represent the visible elements, materials and applications applied to a building's interior excluding furniture, fixtures and equipment. (See FF&E)

Invoice A list sent to a purchaser containing the items and charges of merchandise. (See Statement)

Isolation Valve A valve that allows a specific section of a system to be shut off for maintenance without disrupting the entire building.

Labor and Material Payment Bond (1) A written form of security from a surety (bonding) company to the owner, on behalf of an acceptable prime or main contractor or subcontractor, guaranteeing payment to the owner in the event the contractor fails to pay for all labor, materials, equipment, or services in accordance with the contract. (see Performance Bond and Surety Bond)

Latent Defect A hidden flaw in construction that is not discoverable through normal inspection and may appear months or years after completion.

Leasehold Improvements A term used to mean *Tenant Improvements*. Generally, this term is used when building in retail stores as contrasted with the term *Tenant Improvements* which are generally associated with office buildings. The terms are often used interchangeably. (See TI'S)

Lien, Mechanic's or Material The right to take and hold or sell an owner's property to satisfy unpaid debts to a qualified contractor for labor, materials, equipment or services to improve the property. (See Preliminary Lien Notice)

Lien Release A written document from the contractor to the owner that releases the Lien, Mechanic's or Material following it's satisfaction.

Lien Waiver (1) A written document from a contractor, subcontractor, material supplier or other construction professional(s), having lien rights against an owner's property, relinquishes all or part of those rights. (2) Lien waivers are generally used for processing progress payments to prime or main or subcontractors as follows: Conditional Lien Waiver, Unconditional Lien Waiver, and Final Lien Waiver.

Life-Cycle Cost The total cost of owning, operating, maintaining, and replacing a system over its useful life—not just the initial purchase price.

Limited Common Elements Common areas reserved for the exclusive use of specific units, such as balconies, lanais, or assigned parking stalls.

Liquidated Damages A pre-agreed monetary amount the contractor must pay for each day the project is delayed beyond the contract completion date.

Long-Lead Items Materials or equipment with extended manufacturing or delivery times that must be ordered early to avoid schedule delays.

Low-VOC Materials Products that emit minimal volatile organic compounds, improving indoor air quality and occupant health.

Lump Sum Agreement (See Stipulated Sum Agreement)

Lump Sum Bid A single entry amount to cover all labor, equipment, materials, services, and overhead and profit for completing the construction of a variety of unspecified items of work without the benefit of a cost breakdown.

Lump Sum Contract A written contract between the owner and contractor wherein the owner agrees the pay the contractor a specified sum of money for completing a scope of work consisting of a variety of unspecified items or work.

Meeting Attendance Form A form consisting of three columns (individuals name, individuals title, and company the individual represents). This form is given to all persons attending any meeting. Each person attending the meeting will fill in their respective information. The date of the meeting should be included for reference.

Meeting Notes A written report consisting of a project number, project name, meeting date and time, meeting place, meeting subject, a list of persons attending, and a list of actions taken and/or discussed during the meeting. Generally, this report is distributed to all persons attending the meeting and any other person having an interest in the meeting.

Milestone An activity with a duration of zero (0) and by which progress of the project is measured. A milestone is an informational marker only; it does not affect scheduling.

Owner (1) An individual or corporation that owns a real property.

Owner-Architect Agreement A written form of contract between architect and client for professional architectural services.

Owner's Representative A professional engaged to protect the owner's interests by overseeing scope, cost, schedule, quality, and communication.

Owner-Builder A term used to describe an *Owner* who takes on the responsibilities of the general contractor to build a specific project.

Owner-Construction Agreement Contract between owner and contractor for a construction project.

Owner-Construction Management Agreement Contract between construction manager and client for professional services.

Performance Bond (1) A written form of security from a surety (bonding) company to the owner, on behalf of an acceptable prime or main contractor or subcontractor, guaranteeing payment to the owner in the event the contractor fails to perform all labor, materials, equipment, or services in accordance with the contract. (2) The surety companies generally reserve the right to have the original prime or main or subcontractor remedy any claims before paying on the bond or hiring other contractors. (See Labor and Material Payment Bond and Surety Bond)

Performance Specifications The written material containing the minimum acceptable standards and actions, as may be necessary to complete a project. Including the minimum acceptable quality standards and aesthetic values expected upon completion of the project.

PERT An abbreviation for Program Evaluating and Review Technique. (See Activity; Critical Path Method)

PERT Schedule A diagram that illustrates, charts and reports a projects estimated start and completion times; and work in progress.

Plan (1) A line drawing (by floor) representing the horizontal geometrical section of the walls of a building. The section (a horizontal plane) is taken at an elevation to include the relative positions of the walls, partitions, windows, doors, chimneys, columns, pilasters, etc. (2) A plan can be thought of as cutting a horizontal section through a building at an eye level elevation.

Plan Checker A term sometimes used to describe a building department official who examines the building permit documents.

Planner A person who forms a scheme or method for doing something; an arrangement of means or steps for the attainment of some object; a scheme, method, design; a mode of action.

Plans A term used to represent all drawings including sections and details; and any supplemental drawings for complete execution of a specific project.

Pre-Construction Planning and Team Building A process used for the purpose of establishing below market dollar budget(s), overall project scheduling and design criteria; also identification and selection of the most feasible planning, design and construction team.

Predecessor An activity that must be completed before another activity can begin.

Preliminary Drawings (1) The drawings that precede the final approved drawings. (2) Usually, these drawings are stamped or titled “PRELIMINARY”; and the “PRELIMINARY” is removed from the drawings upon being reviewed and approved by the owner.

Preliminary Lien Notice A written notice given to the property owner of a specific project by the subcontractors and any person or company furnishing services, equipment or materials to that project. The notice states if bills are not paid in full for the labor, services, equipment, or materials furnished or to be furnished, a mechanic's lien leading to the loss, through court foreclosure proceedings, of all or part of the property being so improved may be placed against the property even through the owner has paid the prime contractor in full. The notice explains how the owner can protect himself against this consequence by (1) requiring the prime contractor to furnish a signed release by the person or firm thus giving the owner notice before making payment to the prime contractor or (2) any other method or device which is appropriate under the circumstances. The state of California mandates that a *Preliminary Lien Notice* must be given to the property owner not more than 20 days after starting the work on the specific project.

Pre-qualification of prospective bidders A screening process wherein the owner or his/her appointed representative gathers background information from a contractor or construction professional for selection purposes. Qualifying considerations include competence, integrity, dependability, responsiveness, bonding rate, bonding capacity, work on hand, similar project experience, and other specific owner requirements.

Pressure-Reducing Valve (PRV) A valve that lowers incoming water pressure to a safe, consistent level for building systems and fixtures.

Pressure Zone A vertical section of a high-rise building served by its own pressure-controlled water distribution system.

Preventive Maintenance Plan A structured program of scheduled inspections and service tasks designed to extend the life of building systems and reduce failures.

Preventive Maintenance Schedule The calendar of specific maintenance tasks, frequencies, and responsibilities derived from the preventive maintenance plan.

Prime Contract A written contract directly between a prime or main contractor or subcontractor for work on a specific project.

Prime Contractor (1) Any contractor having a contract directly with the owner. (2) Usually the main (general) contractor for a specific project.

Principal (1) The leading participant of professional practice.

Professional Engineer One who is professionally engaged in a branch of engineering.

Program An ordered list of events to take place or procedures to be followed for a specific project.

Progress Payment A payment from the owner to the contractor determined by calculating the difference between the completed work and materials stored and a predetermined schedule of values or unit costs. (See Schedule of values; Unit Costs).

Progress Schedule A line diagram showing proposed and actual starting and completion times the respective project activities. (See Activity)

Progress Verification An owner's or representative's confirmation that completed work matches the claimed percentage before approving payment.

Project A word used to represent the overall scope of work being performed to complete a specific construction job.

Project Cost All costs for a specific project including costs for land, professionals, construction, furnishings, fixtures, equipment, financing and any other project related costs.

Project Directory A written list of all parties connected with a specific project. The list usually includes a classification or description of the party (i.e., Owner, Architect, Attorney, General Contractor, Civil Engineer, Structural Engineer, etc.); name, address, telephone and FAX numbers opposite their respective classifications or description. It is particularly important that the emergency or after hour telephone numbers are included. These numbers should be kept confidential if requested by the respective parties.

Project Directory on Constructionplace.com A term on Constructionplace.com that means using a form containing fields for Resource Names, Company Name, Profession, Trade/Specialty, and Telephone Number and Email links. When Constructionplace.com Service Providers are added to the directory their complete credentials, insurance information, terms, portfolio and reviews are available. The directory works in tandem with Constructionplaceplace.com on-line Work Reports and Schedule of Values.

Project Manager (Project Management) A qualified individual or firm authorized by the owner to be responsible for coordinating time, equipment, money, tasks and people for all or specified portions of a specific project. (see Construction Manager)

Project Manual A organized book setting forth the bidding requirements, conditions of the contract and the technical work specifications for a specific project. (See Specifications)

Project Representative A qualified individual authorized by the owner to assist in the administration of a specific construction contract.

Project Site (see Site)

Proposal A written offer from a bidder to the owner, preferably on a prescribed proposal form, to perform the work and to furnish all labor, materials, equipment and/or services for the prices and terms quoted by the bidder. (See Bid)

Proposal Form (See Bid Form)

Purchase Order A written document from a buyer to a seller to purchase materials, services, equipment or supplies with acceptable purchase terms indicated.

Punch List (See Inspection List)

Punchlist Turnover The process of identifying, correcting, and verifying minor incomplete or defective items before final acceptance.

Qualified An individual or firm with a recognized degree, certificate, or professional standing; or who by extensive knowledge, training and experience, has successfully demonstrated his/her abilities to identify and solve or resolve problems associated with a specific subject matter or project type.

Record Drawings (See As-Built Drawings)

RFP (1) An abbreviation for Request for Proposal. (2) A written request from the requestor (usually the owner or a contractor) to a contractor, design professional or subcontractor for an estimate or cost proposal. The RFP usually contains a specific scope of work.

RFP on Constructionplace.com A term used on Constructionplace.com means on-line fillable and savable forms, for any size project, for Sending RFPs to selected bidders

(Closed Bid) or to public bidders (Open Bid). This RFP form has a Quick Bid option that allows bidder(s) to simply enter a bid amount and return the bid instantly to the RFP originator. Bid type options are Lump Sum (Fixed Price), Time and Materials, Not to Exceed, and Other. A Messaging application is included for fast and easy communication during the bidding process. And Bids can be declined, negotiated, withdrawn or accepted.

Release of Lien A written action properly executed by and individual or firm supplying labor, materials or professional services on a project which releases his mechanic's lien against the project property. (See Mechanic's Lien)

Reimbursable Expenses (or Costs) Amounts expended for or on account of the project, which in accordance with the terms of the appropriate agreement, are to be reimbursed by the owner.

Reserve Study A long-term financial analysis that identifies major future repairs and replacements and recommends funding levels.

Resident Architect An architect permanently assigned at a job site who supervises the construction work for the purpose of protecting the owner's interests during construction.

Resident Engineer (inspector) An individual permanently assigned at a job site for the purpose of representing the owner's interests during the construction phase. (See Owner's Inspector)

Retro-Commissioning (RCx) is the systematic testing and optimization of existing building systems to restore them to proper, efficient, and reliable performance after years of operational drift. It focuses on identifying issues such as failed sensors, incorrect setpoints, stuck dampers or valves, and improper control sequences, then correcting them without major capital replacement. RCx improves comfort, reduces energy waste, extends equipment life, and updates operating procedures so systems run as originally intended.

R.F.I. (1) An abbreviation for Request for Information. (2) A written request from a contractor to the owner or architect for clarification or information about the contract documents following contract award.

Riser A vertical pipe or conduit that distributes water, waste, air, or electrical services between floors.

Risk Register A project document that identifies potential risks, assigns responsibility, and tracks mitigation actions.

Roll Out A loose term used to describe the rapid succession (completion) of similar projects over a given time period.

Safety Report The Occupational Safety and Health Act of 1970 clearly states the common goal of safe and healthful working conditions. A Safety Report is prepared following a regularly scheduled project safety inspection of the specific project.

Schedule A plan for performing work or achieving an objective.

Schedule of Values A statement furnished by the contractor to the architect or engineer reflecting the portions of the contract sum allotted for the various parts of the work and used as the basis for reviewing the contractor's applications for progress payments.

Schematic A preliminary sketch or diagram representing the proposed intent of the designer.

Schematic Design Phase The first phase of the architect's basic services in which the architect consults with the owner to ascertain the requirements of the project and prepares schematic design studies consisting of drawings and other documents showing the scale and project components for the owner's approval.

Scheme (1) A chart, a diagram, or an outline of a system being proposed (2) An orderly combination of related construction systems and components for a specific project or purpose.

Scope Creep Uncontrolled expansion of project scope without corresponding adjustments to budget, schedule, or contract terms.

Scope of Work A written range of view or action; outlook; hence, room for the exercise of faculties or function; capacity for achievement; all in connection with a designated project. (See Performance Specifications)

Slack Time The flexibility with non-critical jobs that allows their start dates to be adjusted without affecting the project completion date.

Shutoff Zone A defined area of a building that can be isolated from water service using valves for maintenance or emergencies.

Shell & Core A building delivered with its structural frame, exterior envelope, and base systems installed, but interior spaces unfinished.

Site The place where a structure or group of structures was, or is to be located (a construction site).

Soft Costs Soft Costs are cost items in addition to the direct Construction Cost. Soft Costs generally include architectural and engineering, legal, permits and fees, financing fees, construction Interest and operating expenses, leasing and real estate commissions, advertising and promotion, and supervision. (See Construction Cost)

Specifications A detailed, exact statement of particulars, especially statements prescribing materials and methods; and quality of work for a specific project. The most common arrangement for specifications substantially parallels the CSI (Construction Specification Institute) format. (See CSI)

Special Assessment A one-time charge to owners to fund major repairs, emergencies, or capital improvements not covered by reserves.

Special Conditions A section of the conditions of the contract, other than the General Conditions and Supplementary Conditions, which may be prepared for a particular project. Specific clauses setting forth conditions or requirements peculiar to the project under consideration, and covering work or materials involved in the proposal and estimate, but not satisfactorily covered by the General Conditions. (See General Conditions)

Standard Details A drawing or illustration sufficiently complete and detailed for use on other projects with minimum or no changes.

Standard Dimension A measurement unique to a specific manufactured item.

Standards of Professional Practice A listing of minimum acceptable ethical principles and practices adopted by qualified and recognized professional organizations to guide their members in the conduct of specific professional practice.

Standpipe System A vertical fire-protection system that provides water to hose connections on each floor for firefighting.

Start Date The date that an activity or project begins.

Statement A copy or summary of any account covering a stated period. (See Invoice)

Statute of Limitations The period of time in which legal action must be brought for an alleged damage or injury. The period commences with the discovery of the alleged damage or injury; or in construction industry cases with completion of the work or services performed. Legal advice should be obtained.

Stipulated Sum Agreement A written agreement in which a specific amount is set forth as the total payment for completing the contract. (See Lump Sum Contract)

Structural Design A term used to represent the proportioning of structural members to carry loads in a building structure.

Structural Systems (frames) The load bearing assembly of beams and columns on a foundation. The beams and columns are generally fabricated off site and assembled on site. Other systems such as non-load bearing walls, floors, ceilings and roofs are generally constructed within and on the structural system.

Structure (1) Something constructed (2) A building put together based on specific plans and specifications.

Sub An abbreviation for Subcontractor.

Subcontract A written form of agreement between the prime or main contractor and another contractor or supplier for the satisfactory performance of services or delivery or material as set forth in the plans and specifications for a specific project.

Subcontractor A qualified subordinate contractor to the prime or main contractor.

Subcontractor Bond A written document from a subcontractor given to the prime or main contractor by the subcontractor guaranteeing performance of his/her contract and payment of all labor, materials, equipment and service bills associated with the subcontract agreement.

Sublet To subcontract all or a portion of a contracted amount.

Substantial Completion (See Date of Substantial Completion)

Substantial Completion Certificate A formal document confirming that the project is sufficiently complete for occupancy, subject to remaining punch list items.

Substitution A proposed replacement or alternate offered in lieu of and represented as being equivalent to a specified material or process.

Substructure The supporting part of a structure; the foundation.

Sub-subcontractor An individual or firm having a written contract with a subcontractor to perform a portion of the work.

Sub-surface Investigation (1) A term used to represent an examination of soil conditions below the ground. (2) Investigations include soil borings and geotechnical laboratory tests for structural design purposes.

Successor (1) One that succeeds another (2) A scheduled activity whose start depends on the completion of one or more predecessors.

Superstructure The part of a building or other structure above the foundation.

Supervision (1) The act, process, or function of supervising construction materials, methods and processes for a specific project (2) Hands on field direction of the contracted work by a qualified individual of the contractor.

Supplemental Conditions (See Supplementary Conditions)

Supplementary Conditions A written section of the contract documents supplementing and qualifying or modifying the contracts general conditions. (See Conditions of the Contract)

Supplier An individual or firm who supplies and/or fabricates materials or equipment for a specific portion of a construction project but does not perform any labor on the project. (See Vendor)

Surety (see Bonding Company)

T&M (1) An abbreviation for a contracting method called Time and Materials (2) A written agreement between the owner and the contractor wherein payment is based on the contractor's actual cost for labor, equipment, materials, and services plus a fixed add-on amount to cover the contractor's overhead and profit.

Tenant Improvement (Fit-Out) Construction work performed to customize a leased space to meet a tenant's functional and aesthetic needs.

Tenant's Rentable Square Feet Usable square feet plus a percentage (the core factor) of the common areas on the floor, including hallways, bathrooms and telephone closets, and some main lobbies. Rentable square footage is the number on which a tenant's rent is usually based.

Tenant's Usable Square Feet The square footage contained within the demising walls. (See Demising Walls)

TI'S (Tenant Improvements) TI'S is a term used to define the interior improvements of the project after the Building Envelope is complete. TI'S usually include finish floor coverings; ceilings; partitions; doors, frames, hardware; fire protection; HVAC consisting of branch distribution duct work, control boxes, and registers; electrical consisting of lighting, switches, power outlets, phone/data outlets, exit and energy lighting; window coverings; general conditions; and the general contractor's fee. The cost of tenant improvements are generally born by the tenant and the costs of tenant improvements will vary with every building, and with tenant requirements. (See Work Letter)

Time (as time of the essence associated with a construction contract) A provision in a construction contract by the owner that punctual completion within the time limits or periods in the contract is a vital part of the contract performance and that failure to perform on time is a breach and the injured party is entitled to damages in the amount of loss sustained.

Time-and-a-half A term meaning any individuals normal billing hourly rate is increased by a multiple of 1.5 following predetermined normal working hours.

Timely Completion Completing the work of the contract before the date required.

Time of Completion The date or number of calendar or working days stated in the contract to substantially complete the work for a specific project. (See Date of Substantial Completion)

Transmittal A written document used to identify information being sent to a receiving party. The transmittal is usually the cover sheet for the information being sent and includes the name, telephone/FAX number and address of the sending and receiving parties. The sender may include a message or instructions in the transmittal. It is also important to include the names of other parties the information is being sent to on the transmittal form.

Transparency Standards Policies requiring open communication, accessible records, and clear decision-making to maintain owner trust.

Travel Time Wages paid to workmen under certain union contracts and under certain job conditions for the time spent in traveling from their place of residence to and from the job.

Underwriter's Laboratories Label (UL) A label on a product or manufactured item showing the material is regularly tested by, and complies with the minimum standards of the Underwriter's Laboratories specification for safety and quality.

U.B.C. (Uniform Building Code) The Uniform Building Code is one of the family of codes and related publications published by the International Conference of Building Officials (ICBO) and other organizations, such as the International Association of Plumbing and Mechanical Officials (IAPMO) and the National Fire Protection Association (NFPA), which have similar goals as far as code publications are concerned. The Uniform Building Code is designed to be compatible with these other codes, as together they make up the enforcement tools of a jurisdiction.

Uniform System (See CSI Format)

Unit Price Contract A written contract wherein the owner agrees to pay the contractor a specified amount of money for each unit of work successfully completed as set forth in the contract.

Unit Prices A predetermined price for a measurement or quantity of work to be performed within a specific contract. The designated unit price would include all labor materials, equipment or services associated with the measurement or quantity established.

Value Engineering A structured review to reduce cost while maintaining required function, performance, and quality.

Verbal Quotation A written document used by the contractor to receive a subcontract or material cost proposal over the telephone prior to the subcontractor or supplier sending their written proposal via mail or facsimile.

Vendor One that sells materials or equipment not fabricated to a special design.

Vent Stack A vertical pipe that allows sewer gases to escape and maintains proper air pressure in the drainage system.

Warranty Period The time after project completion during which the contractor must repair defects in materials or workmanship.

Water Efficiency The use of fixtures, systems, and practices that reduce water consumption without compromising performance.

Water Hammer A sudden pressure surge caused by rapid valve closure or pump shutdown, which can damage pipes and equipment.

Wet Stack A vertical pipe that carries water under normal operation, such as a supply or waste line.

Work Authorization A written approval allowing the contractor to proceed with specific work, often used for changes or additional tasks.

Work The successful performance of the entire scope of the project being performed for a specific construction project including labor, materials, equipment, and other associated items necessary to fulfill all obligations under the contract.

Working Drawing A drawing sufficiently complete with plan and section views, dimensions, details, and notes so that whatever is shown can be constructed and/or replicated without instructions but subject to clarifications. (See Drawings)

Work Order A written order, signed by the owner or his representative, of a contractual status requiring performance by the contractor without negotiation of any sort.

Work Letter A written statement (often called Exhibit B to a lease or rental agreement) of the specific materials and quantities the owner will provide at his own expense. The work letter defines the building standards, including the type of ceiling, the type and number of light fixtures, the size and construction of the suite-entry and interior doors. Building standards define the quality of tenant spaces. Generally, a Work Letter is associated with the leasing or renting of office space by a tenant within a Building Envelope. (See TI'S and Building Envelope)

Zoning Restrictions of areas or regions of land within specific geographical areas based on permitted building size, character, and uses as established by governing urban authorities.

Zoning Permit A document issued by a governing urban authority permitting land to be used for a specific purpose.

Table of Forms & and Checklists

A Tools, Worksheets & Checklists

B Sample Forms & Templates

C. Courses & Education

www.ingramcontent.com/pod-product-compliance
Lightning Source LLC
LaVergne TN
LVHW061241100826
845148LV00008B/1005

* 9 7 8 0 9 6 6 8 2 4 5 2 0 *